MELODIES MUTED

THE LIVES OF THE FRINGES

EMBERLEAF EDITIONS

Contents

Contents

Melodies Muted: The Lives Of The Fringes

CHIEF-EDITORS

Dr.M.Ratchagar,
Lecturer in English,
Government Polytechnic College,
Kooduveli, Cuddalore.

Dr.K.Thayalamurthy,
Head & Assistant Professor in English,
Government Arts and Science College,
Thiruvennainallur, Villupuram.

CO-EDITORS

Mr.N.Subramaniyan,
Assistant Professor of English,
Arifa Institute of Technology,
Esanoor, Nagapattinam.

Mrs.S.Kalaiselvi,
Lecturer in English,
Government Polytechnic College,
Villupuram.

Preface

The ensuing collection seeks to excavate and amplify voices that have long remained submerged beneath the dominant currents of literary and cultural discourse. It emerges from a commitment to interrogate and deconstruct the hegemonic frameworks that have historically marginalized and silenced individuals and communities based on caste, creed, gender, sexuality, and race. At the heart of this work lies a paradox—the paradox of suppressed expression—wherein voices rich with stories, struggles, and songs have remained unheard, eclipsed by systemic oppression and canonical exclusions.

This scholarly endeavour brings together a diverse array of academic essays that critically engage with questions of representation, resistance, and reclamation. The contributors to this volume explore a wide spectrum of themes, including Dalit writing, LGBTQ+ narratives, caste and communal hierarchies, gendered injustice, and racial discrimination. These essays do not merely highlight the plight of the marginalized; they foreground their agency, resilience, and the urgency of their narratives in shaping an inclusive literary landscape.

The objective of this edited volume is to foreground alternative epistemologies and modes of expression that challenge dominant literary paradigms. In doing so, it contributes meaningfully to contemporary debates on decoloniality, intersectionality, and social justice, offering both theoretical insights and grounded perspectives. This compilation is envisioned as a resource for scholars, students, educators, and activists who seek to engage with literature not merely as an aesthetic form but as a site of critical inquiry, resistance, and transformation.

We are indebted to the contributors for their rigorous scholarship, to the publishing team for their support and meticulous work, and to the communities whose lived realities continue to inspire intellectual and ethical reflection. I hope that this volume will catalyze further discourse, action, and the continued democratization of literary spaces.

-Editors

CHAPTER ONE

Beyond Borders: Identity and Displacement in the Literature of Indian Diaspora

N. Srinivasan[1],
Ph.D. Research Scholar,
Department of English,
Annamalai University.
Dr. S. Florence[2],
Professor,
Department of English,
Annamalai University.

Abstract

This article examines the complexities of belonging and self-definition in a globalized world through the lens of Indian diasporic literature. By analyzing the works of writers such as Jhumpa Lahiri, Arundhati Roy, and Salman Rushdie, it explores the lived experiences of displacement, identity, and cultural negotiation that shape the diasporic experiences. The article delves into the intersections of culture, memory, and the concept of 'home,' highlighting both personal and collective struggles in diasporic life. It discusses how literature captures the tension between cultural preservation and adaptation, as well as the search for rootedness in an interconnected world. Ultimately, the article argues that Indian diasporic writers enrich the literary landscape and serve as cultural intermediaries, offering new insights into both Indian and global identities in the 21st century.

Keywords: Diasporic Experiences, Alienation, cultural identity, displacement.

Beyond Borders: Identity and Displacement in the Literature of Indian Diaspora

The Indian diaspora first began during the colonial period, as the British Empire expanded its influence across the globe, spreading the reach of imperialism to various lands. This migration led to a sense of self-loss among those who moved away from their ancestral homeland. Through writing, many in the diaspora seek to reclaim this lost sense of self. As Dr. T. Deivasigamani notes, "Indian diaspora literature comprises the writings of Indians living in England, the USA, Canada, and other countries, who migrated to improve their economic status, seek employment due to unemployment in their homeland, or pursue better education and career opportunities for their children. Their lives are often marked by hard work" (7).

Diasporic writing in Indian English fiction is a significant genre that captures the experiences and mentalities of the Indian diaspora. It serves as a platform for discussing the lives of Indian immigrants while offering emotional solace to the diasporic community. Female writers, in particular, represent the Indian diaspora effectively, engaging readers with their sensitive and unpretentious style, which resonates with the universal experience of immigration. These writers maintain a connection to both India and the wider world, expressing their expatriate, immigrant, and displaced subjectivities through a stream-of-consciousness style. Their works reflect contemporary realities while delving into the deeper layers of their subconscious minds, shaped by memory, desire, fear, and apprehension. By articulating their sentiments, they not only highlight inner anguish but also universalize the struggles of self-awareness and identity.

Diasporic literature is a broad term encompassing works by individuals living outside their native country while remaining deeply connected to their cultural heritage. Rooted in feelings of alienation and loss due to migration and displacement, this literature reflects the challenges of navigating identity in foreign lands. The Indian diaspora, one of the largest and most diverse in the world, spans multiple continents and is shaped by a variety of historical, social, and cultural influences. Migration, whether voluntary or forced, plays a crucial role in shaping the identities and experiences of these individuals, giving rise to a rich literary tradition.

Indian diaspora literature explores themes of displacement, nostalgia, and the search for belonging, offering a nuanced perspective on identity and cultural heritage.

Through an analysis of select literary works, this study aims to unravel the complexities of diasporic identity and shed light on the diverse experiences of individuals and communities navigating life beyond their homeland. According to Saritha Samuel and Rashmi Pulizala, "Diasporic writings, also known as 'expatriate writings' or 'immigrant writings,' give voice to the traumatic experiences of writers due to cultural clashes and racial discrimination. Expatriate literature primarily explores the inner conflicts arising from cultural displacement. Immigrants, living away from their families, oscillate between crisis and reconstruction, experiencing a threefold alienation: first, from their native land; second, from their host country; and third, from their children" (138).

Diaspora literature remains in constant dialogue with the concept of the meta-home, where the longing for a lost home often results in the creation of a new version of home. Indian diasporic writers have gained global recognition in recent years for their significant contributions to literature. Notable figures include Amitav Ghosh, Salman Rushdie, Kamala Markandeya, Bharati Mukherjee, Chitra Banerjee Divakaruni, Anita Nair, Anita Desai, and Kiran Desai.

Bharati Mukherjee, as an immigrant, grappled with adapting to the traditions, culture, and society of a foreign country, as depicted through the lives of her protagonists Jasmine and Dimple. Her works highlight the challenges of crossing national borders and settling in a new land, revealing themes of resentment, assimilation, belonging, nostalgia, and disappointment. Her collection *The Middleman and Other Stories* explores the impact of cultural displacement, though her work has also faced criticism.

Jhumpa Lahiri is another prominent figure in diasporic literature, known for her nuanced portrayals of immigrant experiences in works like *The Namesake* and *The Interpreter of Maladies*. Her characters, caught between two worlds, resonate with readers, highlighting the struggles of cultural dissonance and the yearning for belonging. Lahiri's exploration of the immigrant psyche and the tension between assimilation and cultural preservation has made her a significant voice in the genre.

Kiran Desai, in her award-winning novel *The Inheritance of Loss*, offers a compelling narrative of displacement and alienation. Set against the backdrop of globalization and economic migration, Desai's work reflects the interconnectedness of disparate lives in an increasingly globalized world. Through characters grappling with displacement and loss, Desai illuminates universal themes of longing for home and the search for meaning amidst upheaval.

Anita Nair, an acclaimed author, has written nine novels, two plays, and a collection of short stories. Her novel *Lessons in Forgetting* explores themes of loss, identity, and resilience within contemporary India. The story follows Meera, a corporate wife whose life unravels after her husband leaves her, and Jak, a cyclone expert searching for answers about his daughter's tragic fate. As their lives intersect, both characters embark on journeys of self-discovery and healing, reflecting on displacement and the strength needed to rebuild one's identity.

Women writers like Chitra Banerjee Divakaruni have paved new paths in diasporic literature, exploring themes of alienation, rootlessness, loneliness, nostalgia, and cultural conflict. Divakaruni's works highlight concerns such as racism, economic disparity, miscarriage, divorce, and homesickness. Her characters, caught between two worlds, often face mental conflict and identity crises as they struggle to retain their homeland's values in a new cultural environment.

Migration and displacement emerge as central themes in Indian diaspora literature, reflecting the experiences of leaving one's homeland and adapting to new cultural landscapes. Authors depict the challenges and opportunities inherent in migration, exploring themes of loss, longing, and the search for identity. Through narratives of migration, Indian diaspora literature highlights the diverse paths taken by individuals and communities in their quest for belonging.

Salman Rushdie, in his seminal work *Midnight's Children*, explores the tumultuous history of postcolonial India and the legacy of partition. His narrative not only delves into the political upheavals of the subcontinent but also interrogates the complexities of individual and national identities in the diaspora. Rushdie's work exemplifies the negotiation of identities, the clash of cultures, and the quest for authenticity that characterize diasporic literature.

The literature of the Indian diaspora stands as a dynamic testament to the resilience and complexity of those navigating the spaces between cultures. It is a rich and evolving tapestry that reflects the complexities of displacement, identity, and belonging. Through diverse narratives, it captures the struggles, aspirations, and cultural negotiations of individuals and communities living between multiple worlds. Whether grappling with nostalgia for a lost homeland, the challenges of assimilation, or the creation of hybrid identities, these voices offer profound insights into the human experience of migration. By exploring themes of memory, cultural retention, and adaptation, diasporic literature not only preserves the essence of Indian heritage but also redefines it within global contexts. Ultimately, these stories affirm that identity is fluid, shaped by personal histories, cultural intersections, and the ever-changing landscapes of migration.

Works Cited

Primary Sources:

Bharati Mukherjee, *Jasmine*. New Delhi, Penguin Books. India, 1990.

Rushdie, Salman. Imaginary Homelands. London, *Granta Books*, 1991.

Lahiri, Jhumpa, *The Namesake*, London: *Harper Collins*, 2010.

Desai, Kiran. *The Inheritance of Loss*, *Grove Press*, New York. 2012.

Secondary Sources:

Deivasigamani,T. *Indian Diaspora Literature*. Chennai. *MJP* Publishers 2022.

Samuel, Saritha. Rashmi Pulizala. "Diaspora in Indian Writings in English: A Study." *International Journal of Creative Research Thoughts (IJCRT)*. Vol.11. Issue.3. (2023): 2320-2882.

Pareek, Priyanka. "Negotiating Identities Across Borders: An Exploration of Indian Diaspora Literature". *Journal of Emerging Technologies and Innovative Research*, Vol.11, Issue.4, (2024):131-134.

CHAPTER TWO

From Verses to Revolt: The Political Poetry of Meena Kandasamy

Mrs. S. Kalaiselvi[1],
Lecturer in English,
Government Polytechnic College,
Arakandanallur, Villupuram, TamilNadu.
Dr.M.Ratchagar[2],
Lecturer in Englis,
Government Polytechnic College,
Kooduveli, Cuddalore, TamilNadu.

Abstract

This study examines how Meena Kandasamy's poetry challenges conventional narratives about caste, gender, and language and is a potent form of resistance. Her art reclaims historically underrepresented voices and challenges oppressive social structures. Four core facets of Kandasamy's poetic expression are examined in this study: free verse as a form of rebellion, linguistic defiance against Brahmanical norms, the reinterpretation of Hindu mythology, and Dalit feminism and rage. This essay places Kandasamy's poetry in the broader context of feminist literary activism and Dalit movement by examining it through these lenses. Her poetry is a call for justice, defiance, and revolution that goes beyond simple artistic expression.

Keywords : Dalit feminism, Political Poetry, Subaltern Voice, Intersectionality, Linguistic Rebellion.

From Verses to Revolt: The Political Poetry of Meena Kandasamy

Poetry has always been a potent instrument of resistance, elevating the voices of the oppressed and opposing repressive structures. Poetry has been used as a tool of defiance by poets like Langston Hughes, Audre Lorde, and Pablo Neruda to address issues of political, gender, and racial injustice. Meena Kandasamy carries on this tradition in Indian literature by using her poetry to oppose linguistic elitism, gender oppression, and caste discrimination. Her writings directly challenge the patriarchal, upper-caste systems that have long dominated Indian literature, marking a radical break from conventional literary conventions.

The poetry of Kandasamy is a place of rebellion, an unvarnished expression of anger, fortitude, and defiance. Her poems defy accepted notions of "literary civility," adopting an honest, unreserved style that subverts prevailing narratives. Her collections, including *Touch* (2006) and Ms. Militancy (2010), break down the linguistic barriers that support Brahmanical dominance, reimagine Hindu mythology from a feminist perspective, and reveal the cruelty of caste hierarchies. To show how Kandasamy's poetry functions as both defiance and revolution, this study explores four major themes: linguistic subversion, the reinterpretation of Hindu epics, Dalit feminism and the politics of rage, and her use of free verse.

Rage as Resistance

Stories of victimization and resistance have frequently alternated in Dalit literature. Kandasamy's poetry marks a shift towards defiant rage, whereas earlier Dalit writings, like those by Bama and Omprakash Valmiki, used autobiographical narratives to illustrate the horrors of caste oppression. She presents anger as an active force that fuels resistance rather than portraying Dalits as helpless victims. Dalit literature should be used as a tool of political struggle in addition to documenting suffering, according to Sharmila Rege (2006). This spirit is personified by Kandasamy, who turns her rage into poetic weapons.

Her 2010 collection, Ms. Militancy, is proof of the strength of anger. Since militancy is frequently portrayed as a bad quality that is linked to violence and disturbance, the title alone is important. The phrase is reclaimed by Kandasamy, who portrays militancy as an essential reaction to structural oppression. Her poetry defies politeness; it is direct, fierce, and uncompromising. Her words are not tempered to appeal to an upper-caste readership, nor does she look to the literary establishment for approval. As she puts it in Ms. Militancy,

> "I am not your good woman.
> I do not keep my head bowed.
> I do not hold my tongue."

Dalit feminist philosophy is based on this rejection of submissiveness. Dalit women experience multiple forms of oppression, and Dalit feminism acknowledges the intersection of caste and gender, in contrast to mainstream feminism, which frequently concentrates on gender equality within the established structures (Paik, 2014). This intersectionality is embodied in Kandasamy's poetry, which rejects both casteism and the patriarchal demands for subservience.

Breaking the Chains of Patriarchy

Due to their oppression as women and Dalits, Dalit women hold a special place in society. They experience systemic marginalization, sexual exploitation, and violence based on caste. These experiences are directly addressed in Kandasamy's poetry, which both exposes the cruelty meted out to Dalit women and promotes their agency and resistance.

She discusses how Dalit women's bodies are used as targets of control and violence in Touch (2006). She draws attention to the hypocrisy of a culture that exploits Dalit women in private while treating them as untouchable in public. Ambedkar (1936) referred to this duality as the "graded inequality" of the caste system, which denies Dalits their dignity while leaving them open to exploitation.

But Kandasamy calls for an end to oppression rather than just documenting it. Her poems are a rallying cry for the abolition of patriarchy and caste. She identifies with Ambedkarite philosophy, stressing that structural change is the only way Dalit women can truly be free. Dalit women must oppose patriarchal oppression both within their own communities and in upper-caste society, according to Gopal Guru (1997). Kandasamy's poetry exemplifies this dual resistance by opposing the male-dominated Dalit movement as well as the Brahmanical patriarchy.

Mythology as a Tool of Control

Hindu epics have long served to legitimize caste systems and patriarchal conventions by reaffirming Brahmanical supremacy. While Dalits are either absent or reduced to inferior roles in traditional interpretations of the Ramayana and Mahabharata, women are frequently portrayed as subservient characters. With subversive retellings that restore agency to historically marginalized characters, Kandasamy questions these narratives.

She recasts Kali, Sita, and Draupadi as rebellious rather than submissive characters in Ms. Militancy. Instead of remaining silent in the face of her humiliation, her Draupadi demands justice. Her Sita challenges the validity of patriarchal purity tests rather than merely walking into the fire. The work of feminist scholars like Uma Chakravarti (2003), who contends that mythological narratives have been created from an upper-caste male perspective, is consistent with this reconfiguration of mythology.

Reclaiming Female Agency

As a kind of literary activism, Kandasamy rewrites these tales to show that the past is not unchangeable and can be changed for the sake of justice. Scholars like Sharmila Rege (2013), who support Dalit feminist historical interpretations, are echoed in her poetry. The narratives that have historically silenced or demonized marginalized voices are challenged by Kandasamy's work, which is an act of reclamation.

Linguistic Subversion: Breaking the Chains of Brahmanical Language

In India, caste privilege has long been indicated by language. Sanskrit was traditionally only used by Brahmins, and English continues to be an exclusive language that is mainly used by the wealthier classes. By rejecting the purified, Brahmanical form of English poetry, Kandasamy upends this linguistic hierarchy.

Her poetry is honest, unvarnished, and unreservedly political. She resists the pressure to adhere to the literary standards set by writers from higher castes by combining Tamil and English expressions. Subverting linguistic norms is a crucial component of Dalit resistance, as Anand Teltumbde (2018) contends that language itself can be used as a tool of caste oppression.

Free Verse and Unapologetic Expression

Kandasamy purposefully rejects poetic formalism through the use of free verse. She symbolically escapes the limitations of literary elitism by refusing to conform to strict structures. Her poetry aims to be heard, not to be beautiful. This supports the claim made by Dalit literary critic Sharankumar Limbale (2004) that authenticity should take precedence over artistic sophistication in Dalit literature.

The Power of Raw Expression

Her purposefully raw poetry conveys a sense of urgency and immediacy. Instead of trying to soften her words, she makes sure they hit hard. This rawness refuses to lessen the impact of caste and gender oppression for the sake of literary decorum, reflecting their realities. "Poetry is not a luxury," as Audre Lorde (1984) states. It is essential to our survival. This philosophy is personified by Kandasamy, who employs poetry as a weapon rather than an art form.

Conclusion

Poems by Meena Kandasamy are a literary protest against patriarchy, caste, and linguistic elitism. Through her unreserved anger, radical mythological reinterpretations, linguistic subversion, and rejection of poetic formalism, she challenges India's deeply rooted social hierarchies. Her art is about revolution rather than merely representation. The marginalized voices are not only heard but also felt thanks to Kandasamy's use of poetry as a tool of resistance, upending a literary tradition that has long silenced them.

Works Cited

Ambedkar, B. R. The Annihilation of Caste. Navayana, 1936.

Chakravarti, Uma. Gendering Caste: Through a Feminist Lens. Stree, 2003.

Guru, Gopal, et al. Dalit Women Speak Out: Caste, Class, and Gender Violence in India. Zubaan, 1997.

Kandasamy, Meena. Ms. Militancy. Navayana, 2010.

---. Touch. Peacock Books, 2006.

Limbale, Sharankumar. Towards an Aesthetic of Dalit Literature: History, Controversies and Considerations. Orient Blackswan, 2004.

Lorde, Audre. Sister Outsider: Essays and Speeches. Crossing Press, 1984.

Paik, Shailaja. Dalit Women's Education in Modern India: Double Discrimination. Routledge, 2014.

Rege, Sharmila. Writing Caste, Writing Gender: Narrating Dalit Women's Testimonies. Zubaan, 2006.

Teltumbde, Anand. Republic of Caste: Thinking Equality in the Time of Neoliberal Hindutva. Navayana, 2018.

CHAPTER THREE

Strength of Woman in Bharathi Mukherjee's Jasmine

K. Arivazhagan[1],
Research Scholar,
Government Arts and Science College,
Thiruvennainallur.Villupuram, Tamilnadu.
Dr. K. Thayalamurthy[2],
Assistant Professor and Head,
Government Arts and Science College,
Thiruvennainallur.Villupuram, Tamilnadu.

Abstract:

The study aims at exploring the cultural and psychological conflicts in the minds of Bharathi Mukherjee's woman immigrants while setting down in a foreign country in a new milieu-their problems, anxieties, and miserable plights in the light of present socio-political scenario. One of the significant themes of modern literature is the depiction of the cross-cultural crisis, leading to psychological problems, a subject which has assumed a great significance in present world of globalization. Bharathimukherjee's writing is undoubtedly one of the best examples of this kind. The authors' aim in this paper is to observe, examine and present the existing position of women and the problems they face both in India and abroad. Through the main character, Jasmine, the attempt is made to give a picture of women who suffer from man-made cultural and traditional prescriptions as well as sanctions which do not allow them live a life free from such constraints. The social issues that the protagonist raises are of cosmopolitan significance. The picture that emerges from the study of the novel is not only that of female being victimized by male but also that of female coming out as strong character to combat the challenges that come on her way.   Through the paper the endeavor is to encompass the social and cultural issues through the mouth of a very dominant female character who is successful in bringing about a cultural and social change by presenting her condition in cinematographic manner.

Key words: *Female sexuality, immigrants, criticism, Jasmine, Bharati Mukherjee.*

Strength of Woman in Bharathi Mukherjee's Jasmine
INTRODUCTION:

Strength of Woman in Bharathi Mukherjee's Jasmine

Bharathi Mukherjee is one of the major novelists of Indian diaspora who have archived enviable position within a comparatively short creative span. As an expatriate in the United States, she has captured evocatively the Indian immigrant experience in her novels as well as two collections of short fiction. As she takes up the life of the Indian immigrate in the U.S.A. as the subject-matter of most of her novels. In her novels, she explores the theme of immigration and transformation. The immigrant they undergo a process of adjustment and transformation of their personalities. She journeys through the different phases such as the phase of expatriation, transition and immigration. Her works revel her embattlement with ethos, cultures and people of the country where she was born (India) and the land of her immigration (America). The quality of culture conflict leading to psychological crisis in her fiction in all its multiplicity forms the crux of her accomplishment as a creative artist. She is at her best in the depiction of cultural clash between the east and the west leading to psychological crisis in the inner mind of her protagonists. Mukherjee focuses upon sanative women protagonist who lack stable sense of personal and culture identity. She is curious about the survival of her protagonist in the new surroundings. She is concerned about making her picture of Indian life intelligible and interesting to the American readers.

The contemporary feminist criticism is the historical outgrowth of the feminist movement that began in the 1960s and continues to flourish into the twenty-first century. Like their predecessors, the contemporary feminists explore the relationship between gender and language and the issues of both overt and tacit discrimination against women.

In the social structure of World, Women were expected to focus on practical domestic pursuits and activities that encouraged the betterment of their families only, and more particularly, their husbands. In most cases education for women was not advocated, it was thought to be detrimental to the traditional female virtues of innocence and morality. Women who spoke out against the patriarchal system of gender roles or any injustice ran the risk of being exiled from their communities, or worse; unmarried women in particular were the targets of witch-hunts. Because of this great gender inequality and somewhat non-uniform social hierarchy, male and female, in spite of becoming two individuals, have been caste as two different cultural beings having utterly different life experiences. In this reference the comments of a great writer, Simone de Beauvoir throws light on the condition of the fairer sex in the society:

Female sexuality is not seen as a personal or private matter, but a family concern whether it is marriage, education or any other activity associated with their lives. Feminism is a reaction against the gender biasness. It is an attempt to throw a challenge on the age-long tradition of gender differentiation and to analyze, comprehend and clarify how and why the feminine sensibility is different from masculinity or masculine experiences treating them as two equal individuals. As democracy is of the people, for the people and by the people, so feminism can also be interpreted as a people movement - of, by, and for the females. Feminism looks into the relationship between men and women with a new insight through literature in the form of visionary reinterpretation of writings by men and their effects on women, representation of women in the texts, texts by women and women's portrayal of men and their reaction towards the gender roles. So feminism with its main thrust on gender and sexuality plays a vital role in studying the construction of masculine and feminine identities. So in literary texts, Feminism brings to scrutiny the portrayals of gender roles, which tend to impose social norms, customs, conventions, laws and expectations on the grounds of gender discrimination. In this context, Suswhila Singh, a critic on feminist literature, observes that:

The purpose of this paper is to admire Bharati Mukherjee's spirit of celebration of strength of women. It is also an attempt to have a deep insight into the life of the protagonist and put forward her multi-dimensional pathetic and rebellious feminist emergence from village girl Jyoti to Americanized Jasmine of the new World and to whom Mukherjee has created a model of the fighters, women who have to adopt and struggle for their own survival.

This is the story of Jyoti, an Indian immigrant who is a village girl of Hasanpur in Punjab. Jyoti's childhood was spent in a small village. She being the seventh child of her parents is undesirable and curse for them. It is observed that Jyoti is a very smart, bold and intelligent girl. In fact the novel *Jasmine* is an account of the protagonist's various transformations from Jyoti to Jasmine, from Jase to Jane- and each time we encounter a different woman in her. She is a fighter, a survivor, and an adapter.

In the midst of her traditional village, Hasanpur, Jasmine is in quest for freedom. Her soul longs to fly high in the sky without having any bondage. She rebels against the blind beliefs and superstitions prevailing in her small village and argues against the fate which is adumbrated by the astrologer by saying:

Fate is fate. When Beulah's bridegroom was fated to die of snake bite on their wedding night, did building a still fortress prevent his death? (Mukherjee, 1990:2)

The star shaped wound on her forehead, which she gets while defying the astrologer's prediction about her widowhood and exile is treated as a third eye by her, like those of lord Shiva, and she says that through this third eye she will have a wider and true perspective of life. This assumption of Jyoti definitely reveals the stronger and modern side and also shackles the older rotten notion of Hindu tradition where the fate of a child, from birth till death, dances on the tune of astrologers. Not only this but Jasmine also withdraws all the notions set for the marriage by the society. Bharati Mukherjee shows Jasmine repudiating centuries old ugly Indian tradition of marriage after checking the boy's horoscope. She marries a Christian boy Prakash in the court and from there Jyoti becomes Jasmine-a city woman and wife of a modern man. The heroine's problems do not culminate in the resolution of tying a knot of marriage or walking out of it but to combat the challenges. The emphasis is on the passion for life and an establishment of a woman's right to live and love. The narrative treatment is an attempt to 'defamiliarize' the traditionally accepted image of an Indian woman. The collapse of the heroine's submission to convention, aims to establish her independence.

But, unfortunately, Jasmine's husband, Prakash's life proves to be very short and he falls a prey to the Khalsa Lions, the rebel demanding a separate land of Khalistan for Sikhs.

Her grandmother reproaches her for her modern outlook of her marriage and says:

If you had married a widower in Ludhiana that was all arranged. If you had checked the boy's horoscope and married like a Christian in some government office...if you had waited for a man I picked none of this would have happened...God was displeased. God send that Sardarji boy to do that terrible act (Mukherjee, 1990: 98).

The reaction of Jasmine against this shows the assertive side of the heroine and the strong-willed power of her character. She blazes forth:

Dida, I said, if God send Sukhi to kill my husband and then I renounce God, I spit on him (Mukherjee, 1990: 89).

Jasmine decides to go to America, on forged papers and documents, to burn her as 'sati' in the campus of the same engineering college where her husband was admitted for study, as it becomes clear from the following statement:

A village girl going alone to America without job, husband or papers? (Mukherjee, 1990: 97).

Here we see Jasmine getting attached with the ancient Indian traditional practices where a woman becomes sati after her husband's death. But actually what comes into mind at this course of action is that though Jasmine is a freedom loving woman at global level, yet her heart is purely Indian and it denies continuing the life without the love of her husband. Besides this another thing that comes into light is that she does not want to live the life of a widow and suffer all those that a widow in the society is subjected to. Here we can see the strength of a woman who has decided to move on a perilous journey to the new world to fulfill her husband's dream. Let's hear it in the protagonist's own words:

My husband was obsessed with passing exams, doing better, making something more of his life then Fate intended...If you could first get away from India, then all fates would be cancelled...

We'd be on the other side of the earth, out of God's sight (Mukherjee, 1990: 85).

Here the pain of a woman can be clearly felt who wants to do anything in order to fulfill the last wish of her deceased husband. Jasmine too with the same spirit to fulfill the dreams of her husband leaves for America without having any clue of her forthcoming life.

She travels to New York on a ship, where the captain of the ship, an ugly fellow, half-faced(a nickname as one side of the face was badly damaged in war) who had lost an eye, ear and most of his cheek, remorselessly rapes Jasmine and this outrage is too much for an Indian widow to tolerate. She decides to finish her life but before she could do so, the woman inside her realizes that actually she wants to live and her personal dishonor cannot disrupt her mission. She decides that in spite of ending her life she will destroy the devil that has outraged her chastity. She transforms herself into the image of vengeful goddess Kali. She extends her tongue and slices it; the blood oozing out gives her the perfect image of the goddess of destruction. She kills the demon and for some moment gets perturbed and in this state of mind she reacts:

No one to call to, no one to disturb us. Just me and the man who raped me, the man I had murdered. The room looked like a slaughter house, blood has congealed on my hands, my chin, my breast...I was in a room with a slain man, and my body blooded was walking death, death incarnate (Mukherjee, 1990: 119).

Jasmine's killing of half face is a kind of herself assertion. Her decision to kill herself first is a decision of a woman who lives for her deceased husband but the woman who kills half faced is prompted by her will to live and continue her life facing the challenges that come on her way. She says:

I didn't feel the passionate embrace of lord yama that could turn a kerosene flame into a lover's caress. I could not let my personal dishonor disrupt my mission. There could be a plenty of time to die....i extended my tongue and sliced it (Mukherjee, 1990: 117).

Bharati Mukherjee brilliantly fuses two archetypal images to enact this killing: the one of kali, the goddess of destruction and strength and another of the broken pitcher in which there is no difference between the inside and the outside and "we are just the shells of the same absolute." (p.15).It also symbolizes the death of her older self by the symbolic burning of her dishonored clothes and out of the ashes raises her new self that wants to live. Samir Dayal, a critic on Indian writing, writes that In killing half-faced she experiences an epistemic violence that is also a life time transformation (Dayal, 1993: 71).

The credit goes to Bharati Mukherjee for transforming a village girl into the goddess of strength and showing that women are not meek and submissive but they are strong willed and assertive by nature. Her silence preserves the biggest storm in her and when it comes to personal honor, she, like the goddess, can punish the wrong doer and also kill and finish the biggest demons. She also brings out the agonizing evil side of the society where the other sex becomes demon when it comes to physical gratification. At one place, Jasmine says:

For the first time in my life I understood what evil was about. It was about not being human....It was a very simple, very clear perception, a moment of truth, the kind of understanding that I have heard comes at the moment of death (Dayal, 1993: 116).

She is reborned by the act of killing; to punish the monster in disguise she begins her journey. She had burned herself in the funeral pyre of her clothes behind in a motel in Florida. Here the novelist once again invokes the archetypal image of a broken pitcher and says that the pitcher is broken now and her body, which is merely the shell, is soon to be discarded to get reborned and her soul will find a new habitation:

I said my prayers for the dead clutching my Ganpati. I thought. The pitcher is broken. Lord Yama, who had wanted me, who had courted me, and whom I'd flirted with on the long trip over, had now deserted me...My body was merely the shell, soon to be discarded. Then I could be reborn, debts and sins all paid for (Dayal, 1993: 120-121).

The sanctity about the body is lost and she learns that body is a mere covering, which can be discarded when corrupted.

The setting of the novel is of ninetieth century. The situation of women during this period was that women were expected to remain subservient to their fathers and husbands. Their occupational choices were also extremely limited. The middle- and upper-class women generally remained captive at home, caring for their children and running the household. The lower-class women often did work outside the home, but usually were too poorly-paid domestic servants or laborers in factories and mills. During this time the strong outcome of Jasmine by Bharati Mukherjee was widely accepted by the critics and readers because it showed the assertive side of the female protagonist. Now this feminist of nineties marches on in quest of new identity.

Mrs. Gordon, another strong willed woman who supports and helps her to rehabilitate, transforms her totally. Within a week Jasmine gives up her shy side of personality and dresses up on a jazzy T-shirt, tight cords and running shoes. With the change in clothes comes the change in the culture so much so that the intrinsic qualities of her personality start disappearing. With this change she moves from being a "visible minority" to being just another immigrant. She becomes Jazzy from Jasmine. This adoption of different names and personality is another part of her feminine sensibility. At Vadhera's (Professor of Prakash) place, the freedom loving spirit of Jasmine finds it very difficult to cope with the conservative and "artificially maintained Indianness" (p.145) of them and after spending a few frustrating months she moves to Manhattan and becomes daymummy, a caregiver of Duff, Taylor and Wylie's adopted son. Here she becomes more

Americanized. As a true feminist she does not hold any nostalgia of the dead and buried past .Rather she says:

Let the past make you wary, by all means. But do not let it deform you (Dayal, 1993: 131).

But even after adopting the patters of the dominant culture she maintains the basic traits of Indian culture. For instance ,it is quite unimaginable for her to have a non-genetic childlike Duff and to her it seems a monstrous idea .Again she feels uncomfortable in sleeping alone and Wylie's statement at this totally shocks her: "What you do on your time is your business" (p.172.) Jasmine in spite of many transformations remains an Indian woman from heart and is never bifurcated from her till the last. The stories which she uses to tell Duff were about Indian Gods, demons and mortals and it supports the Indianness of hers. And thus the woman inside her becomes totally shattered when Wylie walks out of Taylor's life and the protagonist comments:

In America nothing lasts can say that now and it doesn't shocks me, but I think it was the hardest lesson of all to learn. We arrive so eager to learn, to adjust, to participate only to find the monuments are plastic, agreements are annulled. Nothing is forever; nothing is so terrible that it won't be disintegrate (Dayal, 1993: 181).

She felt that there was no concept of feeling of shame in this society and comes to realize the liquidity of relationship in America. She is outwitted at Wylie's decision of leaving Taylor for another man in search of real happiness. Here the woman of Jasmine is unable to have an empathy with the women of Wylie. In fact, here her thinking is like that of an Indian woman in American milieu. But in the later part of the novel we see the woman of Jasmine comprehending this course of action of Wylie. During this course of action Jasmine falls in love with Taylor and tells him everything about her past. She is now happy in her family with Taylor and Duff but again her past comes in front of her in the form of Sukhi (her husband's murderer) and she has to run to Iowa.

Jasmine's life in Iowa begins with her chance of meeting with Bud Ripplemayer, who not only gives her a new identity but also a new name - Jane Ripplemayer. Here the change in name is again symbolic. As clay modules according to the hands in which it goes, so is the nature of a woman who willingly or unwillingly imbibes herself according to the place, society and culture. When Jane first met Bud he was a tall, handsome, fifty years old banker, a husband, and father of two children. But after six months he is a crippled divorcee living with an illegal immigrant and an adopted son Du, whom he had brought from the Vietnamese refugee camp. Bud courts her because of her mysterious Indian beauty as she accepts it like:

Bud courts me because I am alien. I am darkness, mystery, inscrutability. The east plunges me into instant vitality and wisdom. I rejuvenate him by being who I am (Dayal, 1993: 200).

She identifies her dreams and wishes with Bud's and sacrifices all her individuality to prove herself to be perfect. But somewhere she was not happy with all this and Taylor's arrival at this is a welcome relief to her. She walks out of Bud's life and now the woman inside her could understand Wylie's course of action of leaving Taylor. This is the final affirmation of a true feminist. Her walking out of Bud's life symbolizes that her free spirited woman wants to fulfill all her unfulfilled dreams. She says:

I am not choosing between men. I am caught between the promise of America and old–world dutifulness (Dayal, 1993: 240).

Here we encounter a changed Jasmine who appears to be a chance taker who moves with her former lover breaking all the silent promises that she had made with Bud, in order to enjoy all the world of new hopes and excitements:

Greedy with wants and reckless from hope (Dayal, 1993: 241).

Thus, in the end, her powerful feminist convictions win and the synthesis between the traditional India and contemporary America, very perfectly brings out the feminist side of the protagonist. She, in the end, thinks about herself and chooses the path where she will find real happiness:

It isn't the guilt that I feel its relief. I realize I have already stopped thinking of myself as Jane. Adventure, risk, transformation: the frontier is pushing indoor through uncaulked windows. Watch me reposition the stars, I whisper to the astrologer who floats cross-legged above my kitchen stove (Dayal, 1993: 240).

The story does not become a pathetic story of an immigrant but explores the 'state-of-the-art expatriation' where the woman aggressively waits for the future without regretting the past. The novel seeks to highlight the human needs which are essential for life and which can be realized only by rising above the cultural conditioning. The compelling urge to live, breaks Jasmine emotionally, physically and culturally like an earthen pot. The lesson is that the things we fight to guard-body, feeling and culture-are as fragile as the pitcher. The shifting of her identity from Jyoti to Jasmine to Jane to Jase is also suggestive of the death of one personality and an emergence of a new one but it does not have negative-implications. The protagonist does not see her Indianness as a fragile identity to be preserved against obliteration. Now it is seen as a set of fluid identities to be celebrated. The recurring reference to the broken pitcher indicates the death of Jasmine's different selves. While talking to Dr. Mary Webb Jasmine admits that as a Hindu she believes in rebirth though with different meaning in time-context. She is reborned many times in the present birth only, for Jasmine has seen that the Indian immigrants live a meaningless life and are forced to bury their native identity. Prof. Vadhera, in the novel, is not a professor but an importer and sorter of human hair which he gets from India through the middlemen from Indian villages. Watching Prof. Vadhera at work makes Jasmine reflect 'A hair from peasant's head in Hasnapur could travel across oceans and save an American meteorologist's reputation. She feels nothing is rooted anywhere. Everything is in motion. The novel reflects the moving identity, moving like an escalator, at the same place again and again and after a certain time will become still.

The Americanization of Jasmine is her liberation, though it hints at breaking of the rigid behavioral norms of the traditional Indian society. Being bold and assertive, still Jasmine as character never delimits the definition of woman as a function. Though In America she takes the support of men such as Prof. Vadhera, Mr. Taylor or the banker Bud Ripplemeyer, she has never subjected herself to their mercy. The only positive step in the direction of establishing her self-hood is that she has exercised her freedom of choice. Mukherjee's women characters act like Americans but they think like Indians. Jasmine reflects a combination of womanism and feminism. The novel supports Bharati Mukherjee's assertion. In totality the novel projects the strength of a woman to fight and adapt to a brave New World and not the damaging effects of immigration. The tale from Jyoti to Jasmine, Kali to Jazzy-Jase and Jane is a long and arduous, eventful and uneven odyssey. The protagonist's name changes according to her geographical shifts. The process of continuous uprooting and re-rooting goes on, and the image is that of the celebration of the feminist protagonist who comes out as a fighter, adapter, and survivor.

Conclusion:

Thus, through the analysis of Bharti Mukhrjee's present novel in particular and the novels of feminist writers, it is observed that the women seek to be emancipated even though poor and independent though bound by age customs and traditions. In short, what is wanted by women everywhere -Indian or otherwise-is the same emancipation for the female as for the male. The aim is to be a whole human being, regardless of difference in sex, color, caste, creed, and country.

<u>Works Cited</u>:

Dayal S (1993). Creating, Preserving Destroying: Voilence in Bharati Mukherjee's Jasmine in Emmanuel S. Nelson, ed. Bharati Mukherjee: Critical Perspectives. New York. Garland Publishing, pp. 71, 85, 89, 97-98, 116-117, 119, 120-121, 131, 200.

Iyengar KR, Srinivasana (1962). Indian Writings in English. Bombay. Asia Publishing House.

Kumar N (2001).The Fiction of Bharti Mukherjee: A cultural Perspective. New Delhi.

Mukherjee B (1990). Jasmine. New Delhi, Penguin, p2.

Nahal C (1991) Feminism in Indian English Fiction in Indian Women Novelists. New Delhi. Prestige, 1: 30.

Nayak MK (2004).A History of Indian English Literature1980-2000-A Critical Survey. Pencraft International.

Nelson ES (1993). Bharti Miukherjee: Critical Perspectives. New York. Garland.

Shivramkrishna M (1982). Indian English Novelist. New Delhi. Sterling.

Singh S (1991) Recent Trends in Feminist Thought in Indian Women Novelists. New Delhi. Prestige, 1: .65.

Singh V (2010). The Fictional World of Bharti Mukherjee. New Delhi. Prestige,

Migration and Social Justice: A Comparative Analysis of "We Need New Names" and Indian Migration due to Caste-Based Oppression

Jeeva Micheal Raj.L[1],
Assistant Professor of English,
Arifa Institute of Technology,
Esanoor, Nagapattinam, Tamilnadu
N.Subramaniyan[2],
Assistant Professor of English,
Arifa Institute of Technology,
Esanoor, Nagapattinam, Tamilnadu

Abstract:

This manuscript presents a critical examination of the complex relationships between migration, poverty, racism, and social injustice. Through a comparative analysis of Noviolet Bulawayo's novel "We Need New Names" and the phenomenon of Indian migration due to caste-based oppression, this research explores the multifaceted push factors driving migration, including poverty, lack of job opportunities, and systemic injustices. By drawing parallels between Darling's experiences in the novel and the real-life struggles of Indian migrants fleeing caste-based oppression, this study highlights the need for inclusive and equitable societies that prioritize social justice and human rights. The manuscript underscores the importance of addressing systemic injustices and promoting social cohesion to prevent forced migration and ensure that individuals can thrive in their home countries. Ultimately, this research aims to contribute to a deeper understanding of the complex intersections between migration, social justice, and human rights.

Keywords: Migration, Social Justice, identity, culture,

Migration and Social Justice: A Comparative Analysis of "We Need New Names" and Indian Migration due to Caste-Based Oppression

To adopt the novel's title "We Need New Names" with a story, consider exploring themes of identity, culture, and belonging. The title suggests that the characters, particularly Darling, need to break free from the imposed identities and labels of their colonial past and create new names and labels that reflect their own experiences and realities. By doing so, they can reclaim their agency and define themselves on their own terms.

The novel "We Need New Names" by NoViolet Bulawayo is a postcolonial novel that explores the complexities of identity, culture, and belonging in the aftermath of colonialism. The novel critiques the legacy of colonialism in Zimbabwe, highlighting the ways in which it has shaped the country's history, culture, and identity. Through the eyes of the protagonist, Darling, the novel examines the tensions between traditional and modern identities, as well as the challenges of navigating multiple cultural identities in a postcolonial world.

"We Need New Names" by NoViolet Bulawayo is a postcolonial novel that explores the complexities of identity, culture, and belonging in the aftermath of colonialism. The novel is set in Zimbabwe and the United States, and it follows the story of Darling, a young Zimbabwean girl who migrates to America. Through Darling's experiences, the novel critiques the legacy of colonialism, the impact of globalization, and the complexities of cultural identity. The novel also explores themes of displacement, belonging, and the search for a new sense of self, highlighting the challenges faced by postcolonial subjects in navigating the complexities of their past, present, and future.

The novel "We Need New Names" by Noviolet Bulawayo explores themes of migration, poverty, racism, and violence through the eyes of a 10 year old Zimbabwean girl named Darling. The story is divided into two parts: Darling's life in her hometown of Paradise, Zimbabwe, and her experiences as a migrant in America.

In the novel "We Need New Names" by NoViolet Bulawayo, Darling's poverty status and dreams about America are intricately linked, reflecting the complex and often fraught relationship between poverty, migration, and the pursuit of a better life. Darling lives in a shantytown called Paradise in Zimbabwe with her mother and friends, where they struggle to make ends meet, and their lives are marked by poverty, hunger, and lack of opportunities. Darling's family is unable to afford basic necessities like food, clothing, and healthcare, and they rely on NGO donations and scraps from the wealthy neighborhood of Budapest to survive. Despite the harsh realities of her life, Darling's imagination is fueled by her desire to escape the poverty and hardship of her life in Zimbabwe, and she dreams of America as a land of plenty, where she can find food, shelter, and opportunities. Her aunt Fostalina, who lives in America, sends her letters and parcels, which fuel her imagination and reinforce her desire to migrate. Darling's dreams about America are also influenced by the media and popular culture, as she watches American TV shows and movies, which portray a luxurious and prosperous lifestyle, and she imagines herself living in a big house, eating plenty of food, and attending a good school. In the novel, America is symbolized as a land of hope, opportunity, and freedom, representing a chance for Darling to escape the poverty and hardship of her life in Zimbabwe and create a better future for herself. However, as Darling migrates to America, she faces new challenges and realities that complicate her dreams and ideals. Darling's poverty status has a profound impact on her dreams about America, as her experiences of hunger, hardship, and lack of opportunities fuel her desire to migrate and create a better life for herself. However, her poverty also limits her access to information and resources, which can lead to unrealistic expectations and disappointments. Overall, Darling's poverty status and dreams about America are intertwined, reflecting the complex and often fraught relationship between poverty, migration, and the pursuit of a better life.

Darling's decision to migrate to America is driven by poverty, harassment, and politics. She faces numerous challenges in her new country, including cultural adaptation, language barriers, and racial discrimination.

The novel highlights the push factors that drive migration, including poverty, lack of job opportunities, and government instability. Darling's story mirrors the experiences of many Indians who migrate to other countries in search of better economic opportunities.

The novel also touches on the theme of racial discrimination, highlighting the historical legacy of slavery and racism in America. Despite facing these challenges, Darling struggles to adapt to her new life in America. The novel suggests that migration is often a last resort for individuals who are forced to leave their homes due to circumstances beyond their control. It emphasizes the need for governments to create an enabling environment that allows citizens to thrive in their home countries, rather than being forced to migrate to other countries in search of better opportunities.

.Similarly, many Indians migrate to other countries due to various push factors, including poverty, lack of job opportunities, and social injustices. One of the significant factors driving Indian migration is the prevalence of racism and casteism within Hinduism. Many individuals from lower castes and marginalized communities face systemic oppression, leading them to seek better opportunities and a more equitable society elsewhere. For instance, the Dalit community, formerly known as "untouchables," has faced centuries of oppression and discrimination within the Hindu caste system. Many Dalits have converted to other religions, such as Buddhism, Christianity, or Islam, in search of equality and social justice. This phenomenon is often referred to as "religious migration."

The experiences of Indian migrants, particularly those fleeing caste-based oppression, parallel Darling's story in many ways. Both involve a quest for better opportunities, equality, and social justice. The novel highlights the challenges faced by migrants, including cultural adaptation, language barriers, and racial discrimination.

In the Indian context, religious migration can be seen as a form of resistance against the oppressive caste system. By converting to another religion, individuals can escape the social and economic constraints imposed by their caste. However, this decision often comes with its own set of challenges, including social ostracism and cultural displacement.

The novel "We Need New Names" and the phenomenon of Indian migration due to racism in Hinduism both underscore the need for inclusive and equitable societies. They highlight the importance of addressing systemic injustices and promoting social cohesion to prevent forced migration and ensure that individuals can thrive in their home countries.

Although the novel "We Need New Names" by NoViolet Bulawayo focuses on the experiences of Zimbabwean immigrants, we can infer some reasons why people might be drawn to settle in America, including the promise of economic opportunities, which is often perceived as a land of economic opportunity, where people can find better-paying jobs, start businesses, and improve their financial stability. Additionally, the United States is renowned for its high-quality education system, research opportunities, and cultural diversity, making it an attractive destination for those seeking personal growth and self-improvement. Furthermore, America is often associated with the ideals of freedom, democracy, and human rights, drawing people from countries with limited opportunities, political instability, or oppressive regimes. The country's cultural diversity and inclusivity also make it a unique blend of tolerance and acceptance, attracting people from various backgrounds who seek to rebuild their lives and find a sense of belonging. For some, America represents a safe haven from conflict, persecution, or violence in their home countries, offering a chance to start anew and rebuild their lives. Many people also settle in America to join family members or friends who have already migrated, seeking to rebuild their social networks and support systems. While these reasons are not explicitly stated in "We Need New Names," they are common motivations for people to migrate to America, and the novel provides a more nuanced and complex portrayal of the immigrant experience, highlighting the challenges, struggles, and ambivalences that come with leaving one's home country and adapting to a new life in America.

In the novel "We Need New Names" by NoViolet Bulawayo, Darling's loss of identity is a pervasive theme that is explored throughout the narrative. Darling's migration to America results in a profound sense of dislocation and disorientation, as she is forced to leave behind her familiar surroundings, language, and customs, which were integral to her sense of identity. As she navigates her new environment, Darling struggles to reconcile her past and present selves, leading to a fragmentation of her identity. Her cultural identity is deeply rooted in her Zimbabwean heritage, but as she adapts to American culture, she begins to experience a cultural identity crisis, torn between her loyalty to her native culture and her desire to assimilate into American society.

This cultural identity crisis leads to feelings of confusion, uncertainty, and dislocation, which are exacerbated by her limited proficiency in English. Language plays a significant role in shaping identity, and Darling's struggles to express herself, understand cultural nuances, and connect with others create a barrier between her and the American culture. Even her name becomes a symbol of her identity fragmentation, as she is forced to adopt a new name, "Kelvin," in America, which represents a dislocation from her past identity. As Darling navigates her new environment, she begins to develop a hyphenated identity, oscillating between her Zimbabwean and American selves, marked by a sense of ambiguity, uncertainty, and dislocation.

Darling's loss of identity has a profound psychological impact on her, as she experiences feelings of dislocation, confusion, and disorientation. Her sense of self is fragmented, and she struggles to reconcile her past and present selves. This psychological impact is a testament to the profound effects of cultural displacement on individual identity and well-being. Through Darling's story, the novel highlights the complexities of identity formation and the challenges faced by migrants and immigrants as they navigate the complexities of cultural displacement.

The novel "We Need New Names" by NoViolet Bulawayo does not specifically focus on Indian migration to America. The novel primarily explores the experiences of Zimbabwean immigrants in the United States, particularly the protagonist, Darling, and her friends.

Indians migrate to America for various political reasons. On one hand, push factors such as lack of economic opportunities, corruption, and poor governance in India drive many to seek better prospects abroad. The Indian economy, despite being one of the fastest-growing in the world, still struggles to provide sufficient job opportunities for its vast population. As a result, many Indians, especially the youth, are forced to look for greener pastures in other countries, including America. Corruption and poor governance are other significant push factors. The lack of transparency and accountability in Indian institutions can make it difficult for individuals to access basic services, leading them to seek better governance and transparency in America.

Limited access to education and healthcare, as well as social and economic inequality, also contribute to the desire to migrate. The Indian education system, despite being one of the largest in the world, still struggles to provide quality education to all its citizens. Many Indians are forced to seek education abroad, with America being one of the most preferred destinations. Similarly, the Indian healthcare system, despite being one of the fastest-growing in the world, still struggles to provide quality healthcare to all its citizens. Many Indians are forced to seek medical treatment abroad, with America being one of the most preferred destinations. Social and economic inequality are other significant push factors. The Indian society, despite being one of the most diverse in the world, still struggles to provide equal opportunities to all its citizens. Many Indians, especially those from marginalized communities, are forced to seek better opportunities abroad.

On the other hand, pull factors such as economic prosperity, cultural and social freedom, and access to quality education and healthcare draw many Indians to America. The American economy, despite being one of the largest in the world, still provides many job opportunities for Indians. Many Indians are drawn to America's strong economy, high standard of living, and attractive career opportunities. Cultural and social freedom are other significant pull factors. America, being one of the most diverse countries in the world, provides many Indians with the freedom to pursue their cultural and social interests. Many Indians are drawn to America's diverse and inclusive society, which values individual freedom and creativity.

To stop or reduce Indian migration to America, the Indian government could consider improving economic opportunities by investing in job creation, skills development, and entrepreneurship support. This could include initiatives such as startup funding, vocational training programs, and infrastructure development projects. Enhancing governance and transparency is also crucial. This can be achieved by implementing anti-corruption measures, simplifying bureaucratic processes, and increasing transparency to improve trust in government and institutions. Additionally, increasing access to education and healthcare can help reduce the incentive to migrate. This can be done by investing in quality education and healthcare infrastructure and implementing policies to increase access to these services for all Indians.

Promoting social and economic equality is also essential. This can be achieved by implementing policies to reduce socisal and economic inequality, including affirmative action programs and social welfare schemes. Finally, encouraging diaspora engagement can also help reduce the need for Indians to migrate. This can be done by engaging with the Indian diaspora community in America to encourage investment, knowledge transfer, and skills sharing. The Indian government could also consider providing incentives for Indians to return home, such as tax breaks, subsidies, and other benefits. By addressing these push and pull factors, the Indian government can reduce the incentive for Indians to migrate to America and promote sustainable development at home.

Indian politicians play a significant role in addressing the issue of Indian migration to America, and while they may not be able to completely stop migration, they can work to create better opportunities in India, thereby reducing the push factors that drive people to migrate. By improving economic opportunities, such as creating jobs, fostering entrepreneurship, and investing in education and skills development, Indian politicians can help reduce the economic incentives for migration. Additionally, addressing brain drain by implementing policies to retain skilled professionals in India, such as offering competitive salaries, research funding, and opportunities for career growth, can also help reduce the brain drain. Furthermore, strengthening diaspora engagement by engaging with the Indian diaspora in the US and other countries can help leverage their skills, expertise, and resources to benefit India's development. The Indian government has already implemented various initiatives to engage with the Indian diaspora, including the Overseas Citizenship of India (OCI) Scheme, Pravasi Bharatiya Divas (PBD), and Pravasi Bharatiya Samman Award, which aim to recognize the contributions of the Indian diaspora and provide them with opportunities to connect with their roots and contribute to India's development. By streamlining migration processes, such as providing clear guidance on visa requirements and application procedures, Indian politicians can also help reduce the stress and uncertainty associated with migration. Ultimately, addressing the root causes of migration, such as poverty, inequality, and lack of access to education and healthcare, can help reduce the pressure to migrate, and Indian politicians have a crucial role to play in this regard.

References:

1.Bhabha, Homi K. The Location of Culture. Routledge, 2012.

2. Bulawayo, NoViolet. We Need New Names: A novel. Hachette UK, 2013.

3. Du Bois, William Edward Burghardt. The Suppression of the African Slave-Trade to the United States of America (The Oxford WEB Du Bois). Oxford University Press, 2014.

4. Gilroy, Paul. The Black Atlantic: Modernity and Double Consciousness. Verso, 1993.

5. Moji, Polo Belina. "New Names, Translational Subjectivities:(Dis) location and (Re) naming in NoViolet Bulawayo's We Need New Names." Journal of African Cultural Studies 27.2 (2015): 181-190.

6. Taylor, Jack. "Language, Race, and Identity in Adichie's Americanah and Bulowayo's We Need New Names." Research in African Literatures 50.2 (2019): 68-85.

7. Bulawayo, N. (2013). We Need New Names. Little, Brown and Company. (Reviewed in) African Studies Review, 56(2), 241-243.

8. Goyal, Y. (2014). The African Diaspora and the American Dream: NoViolet Bulawayo's We Need New Names. Journal of Commonwealth Literature, 49(3), 361-375.

9. Muponde, R. (2015). We Need New Names: A Review. Journal of Literary Studies, 31(1), 147-152.

10. Bulawayo, N. (2013). We Need New Names. Little, Brown and Company.

11. Goyal, Y. (2017). The Cambridge Companion to the Postcolonial Novel. Cambridge University Press. (Chapter 12: "The African Diaspora and the American Dream: NoViolet Bulawayo's We Need New Names")

. Muponde, R. (2018). We Need New Names: Essays on the Postcolonial Novel. Langaa

12. Chakraborty, S. (2018). We Need New Names: A Study of the Immigrant Experience in NoViolet Bulawayo's Novel. Master's thesis, University of Delhi.

13. Moyo, T. (2020). The Representation of the African Diaspora in NoViolet Bulawayo's We Need New Names. Ph.D. dissertation, University of the Witwatersrand.

CHAPTER FIVE

The portrayal of Feminist Consciousness in SudhaMurty's DollarBahu

Dr. P. Mohanraj[1]
Assistant Professor (English)
SRM College of Agricultural Sciences
SRM Institute of Science and Technology.
Baburayanpettai, Chengalpattu.
Dr.T.Johnson[2]
Assistant Professor, Department of English
VLB Janakiammal College of Arts and Science, Coimbatore.

Abstract

SudhaMurty is one of the prominent women writers in Indian English literature. Her writings feature a diverse range of characters placed in various situations. The purpose of this paper is to examine the life journey of a young protagonist as she seeks to find her identity through her feminine consciousness in the context of contemporary Indian society. This paper highlights the turbulent struggles women face, including family conflicts between mothers-in-law and daughters-in-law, and their fight to lead independent lives. It also explores how urban middle-class women, while striving for self-identity, remain deeply rooted in values that emphasize their role in uniting the family, as portrayed in SudhaMurty's*Dollar Bahu.* The paper aims to demonstrate that modern women are more than capable of realizing their goals, much like men. It portrays how Murty's female characters exhibit greater moral and emotional fortitude.SudhaMurty is also successful in questioning and challenging age-old traditional beliefs while striving to awaken the feminine sensibilities of her readers.

Keywords: Feminism, self–identity, sensibility, awareness, expectation, and marital life.

The portrayal of Feminist Consciousness in SudhaMurty's *DollarBahu*

Introduction

Feminism is a socio-political movement aimed at creating equal rights between males and females in political, social, and economic spheres. Feminism strives to establish equal opportunities for both men and women in education, economics, and social matters. Contemporary feminism is a rebellion against the ingrained biases that continue to disadvantage women. This movement addresses not only the rights of women but also the perceptions held by society. Beauvoir in The Second Sex (2011) says "… the woman has alwaysbeen man's dependent if not his slave; the two sexes have nevershared the world in equality" (Beauvoir 29).

Sudha Murty was born in 1950 in Shiggon, North Karnataka, India. She is a prolific writer, a dedicated teacher, and the chairperson of the Infosys Foundation. She is the recipient of the R.K. Narayan Award for Literary Art. Murty has written numerous novels, travelogues, collections of short stories, and children's literature. She is also an Indian feminist writer who writes in both English and Kannada. Her writings reflect keen observation and a deep understanding of human behavior, grounded in truth. Her novels address feminist themes and women's issues. While she does not directly challenge male-dominated society, she uses various characters in her novels to question societal norms. She presents her female characters as more intellectual and mature than their counterparts, as they choose their own paths to lead their lives. Murty also portrays the socio-psychological challenges faced by modern Indian women. Her protagonists are well-educated, resilient, and determined to overcome obstacles, fighting against oppressive conditions and protestingagainst the oppression, and suppression under the mask of patriarchy.

Result and Analysis

Vinuta, the protagonist of the novel, lives in her ancestral home with her uncle, Bheemanna Desai, after the death of her parents. She is pursuing a B.A. and excels in her studies. A highly talented individual, she wins prizes in every competition at college. Skilled in Hindustani music, Vinuta is a typical teenage girl who strives to get along with everyone. She marries Girish, a bank clerk, and moves to Bangalore with his family. Although she adjusts to her new family in every way, she cannot seem to satisfy her mother-in-law, Gouramma. Girish's elder brother, Chandru, marries and settles in the U.S. Vinuta is continuously compared to Chandru's wife, Jamuna, causing her significant stress. This constant pressure gradually takes a toll on her peace of mind and health.

Vinuta leaves Dharward after the death of Bheemanna due to a sudden heart attack. She is helpless, has no support from anyone, and has no place to go. Finally, she gets an offer from her uncle and aunt Indu and Rama Rao lives in Banglore. "She was of marriageable age, with any money of her own and no place to go to" (Dollar Bahu, 29) Though Vinuta has a B.Ed degree, she does not get a job so she starts music class at home and later she joins in a school in Jayanagar. Vinuta meets Girish, a bank clerk at Jeyanagar branch of Canara Bank. Later Girish comes to know that his father Shamanna also works in the same school. However, she gets a marriage proposal from the Girish family and agrees with the proposal. Before her marriage, Vinuta has no parents but lives her life happily. After Vinuta's marriage life, she completely changes and adjuststo Girish's family.Shakun Joshi and Ashok Singh Rao aptly in"Feminist Consciousness and Traditionalism in Dollar Bahu by Sudha Murty" observe about Vinuta:

She was the perfect marriage material, with her role and character seemingly already defined. She was deeply passionate about music and would have loved to make a career out of it. However, she gave up those aspirations upon marrying a man who, in the day-to-day aspects of life, not particularly interested in the arts. It was also noted that she had a hidden, independent streak, evident in her persona as a working woman. She disliked being indebted to anyone, a trait that ultimately attracted Girish to her. (Joshi vol 4)

The first encounter Vinuta faces from her mother-in-law. Gouramma, wants to sell Vinuta'sancestral house in Dharward. She always tries to show off thestatus of her family since her elder son is working in America. Vinuta does not like that idea because she feels very upset because of the attachment to the house. Finally,Girish assures Vinuta not to sell the house. After marriage Vinuta, adjusted to her new family members. She wakes up early and does all her householdwork before going to school. Initially, Gouramma likes the behaviour of Vinuta. "Vinuta's attitude was completely unselfish, and she was always willing to adjust to any situation."(Dollar Bahu 45).Vinuta carefully takes all the responsibility. She makes snacks and coffee for the guest who visits Chandru. She avails leave from school to do the household work for that period.

After Chandru's marriage, Vinuta receives little attention, and they never ask her to go shopping. Vinuta handles all the household preparation work. Gouramma never allows Chandru to buy an expensive sari for Vinuta for their wedding. Vinuta faces new challenges after Chandru's wife enters the household. Gouramma prioritizes money over people. She favors her first daughter-in-law, Jamuna, due to her wealth and jewellery, even referring to her as a 'Mahalakshmi' who has entered the family. As a result, Gouramma begins to humiliate Vinuta. Despite doing all the household chores and responsibilities, Vinuta receives neither appreciation nor recognition from her mother-in-law. Sudha Murthy clearly illustrates how money can alter a person's attitude and lead to the humiliation of others

Gouramma considers Jamuna to be a fortunate daughter-in-law. Before Jamuna's arrival, Gouramma used to praise Vinuta for completing all the household chores, but now such praise is no longer given. Gouramma has completely changed her attitude due to the money and jewelry Jamuna possesses. Katha Pollittquestions the treatment against housewives in her workReasonable Creatures: Essays on Women and Feminism (1994) "people often discuss women's duties to others, as if women were not the primary caregivers in society. However, it was emphasized that no one seems to talk about women's duty of care to themselves." (Pollitt 186). Vinuta has lost her priority in the family due to Jamuna's wealth. Although Vinuta works tirelessly and selflessly for her home, Gouramma believes that money is truly priceless. As a result, Gouramma begins to embarrass Vinuta. Jagannath Mahajan, Mukta. "Value vs.Value: An Axiological Study of Sudha Murty's Dollar Bahu" succinctlyputs: Girish's wife, Vinuta, comes from a poor family and, as a result, is unable to bring a substantial dowry or expensive gifts. Consequently, she is not treated as a "bahu" or "Laxmi," but rather as a maidservant. Despite being virtuous and a working woman, Vinuta is seen as secondary. On the other hand, Chandru's wife, Jamuna, hails from a wealthy family and brings dowry, expensive gifts, and jewelry after marriage. As a result, she is honored as Mahalaxmi by her mother-in-law. Her marriage to Chandru elevates her status, making her a "Dollar Bahu.". (Jagannath Mahajan 25)

Vinuta does all the household work during her pregnancy. Suddenly, Surabhi receives a marriage proposal, but no one asks Vinuta's opinion or suggestions, nor is she even informed about Surabhi's marriage. Sudha Murthy clearly portrays that Vinuta is submissive and cannot escape from her duties. Vinuta reveals details about Surabhi's fiancé, Shekhar, including that he has a relationship with a white girlfriend. Gouramma cannot tolerate Vinuta's words and expresses her anger towards her. She scolds Vinuta severely and accuses her of controlling her husband."Every since you have come to this house, you are trying to keep him under your thumb" (Dollar Bahu 64). Surabhi scolds Vinuta, telling her not to blame everyone with her innocent smile. She informs her father that Vinuta is a cunning woman. Vinuta is deeply hurt by Surabhi's words and cannot hold back her tears. She cannot tolerate Surabhi's harsh remarks. This creates a major conflict in the household, with money playing an evil role. Sudha Murthy vividly portrays how many women, like Vinuta, endure immense suffering, pain, and unspoken domestic violence in their in-laws' homes in India.

Vinuta bravely endures all the insults and suffering. She experiences psychological pressure from her own family members. She remains passive, never involving herself in family matters, and comes to understand the true nature of her mother-in-law and Surbhi. Gouramma fails to recognize Vinuta's pregnancy. The family members give much more importance to Surbhi's marriage than to Vinuta's delivery date. As a result, Vinuta travels to Dharwad for the delivery, where she gives birth to a baby boy. Vinuta realizes that she can no longer tolerate her mother-in-law's attitude. She confides in Chandru, expressing that she is unhappy in the house and that there is always a comparison between her and Jamuna. One day, Gouramma suddenly suffers from chest pain. Vinuta immediately takes leave and accompanies her mother-in-law to the hospital. However, Gouramma continues to fail to understand or appreciate Vinuta's true value, as she remains preoccupied with her plans to go to America.

Vinuta's health deteriorates due to the heavy workload at home. After some time, Jamuna becomes pregnant.Vinuta reflects on how her mother-in-law always treated her differently from Jamuna. Gouramma immediately prepares to go to America to assist Jamuna. "She recalled how they had treated her during her pregnancy: there were no gifts, no sweets, and not even a kind word" (77). When Vinuta learns that her mother-in-law is returning from America, she realizes that once again, there will be constant comparisons, and she will receive no support from her husband, Girish. As a result, Vinuta has to endure her mother-in-law's praises for Jamuna. This leads Vinuta into another bout of depression. She also fears that Gouramma will continue to compare her son with Manasi. Vinuta despises the word "dollar" and the entire concept behind it. She wishes to escape this situation and the ongoing comparisons. Shamana advises Vinuta to avoid staying in the house in a state of servitude and urges her to go to Dharwad to live a happy and peaceful life. Heeding her father-in-law's advice, Vinuta decides to settle in Dharwad. Vinuta's departure from her mother-in-law's home marks the beginning of her journey toward establishing her own identity and living independently, free from the bondage of her mother-in-law and the concept of "dollar." Gouramma fails to recognize Vinuta's love and affection, which prompts Vinuta to search for her own identity. The novel concludes with a sense of regret, as Gouramma, Vinuta's mother-in-law, comes to the realization that dollar alone cannot provide true love and affection. However, she fails to recognize the pure soul of her daughter-in-law, Vinuta

Conclusion

Sudha Murty portrays the plight and survival of women through the character of Vinuta in Dollar Bahu. She illustrates how money and the allure of dollars can change a person's character, and attitude, and lead to mistreatment of others in the family. The character of Vinuta, who conforms to the ideology of her mother-in-law, serves as an excellent illustration of the feminine perspective on the female gender. Sudha Murty, also succeeds in questioning and challenging outdated traditional beliefs, while attempting to awaken the feminine sensibilities of her readers. In doing so, she lays the groundwork for a significant cultural shift, advocating for the assertion of the feminine self and paving a new path by highlighting the character of Vinuta.

WorksCited

Beauvoir, Simone de. *The Second Sex. France: Harmondsworth*: Penguin, 1953,1972,1983.

Jagannath Mahajan, Mukta. "Value vs. Value: An Axiological Studyof Sudha Murthy's Dolla Bahu" Literary Endeavour, ISSN 0976-299X. Vol. IX, Issue 1, January, 2018.

Joshi, Shakun and Ashok Singh Rao. *Feminist Consciousness andTraditionalism in Dollar Bahu.* International Journal of English,Literatureand Social Sciences (IJELS)

Murty, Sudha. Dollar Bahu. New Delhi: Penguin, 2003.

Pollitt, Katha. Reasonable Creatures: *Essays on Women and Feminism. Great Britain: Vintage*: The Guernsey Press Co. Ltd, 1995.

CHAPTER SIX

The Intersection of Ambition, Family Expectations, and Individual Identity in Aravind Adiga's Selection Day

Mr. S. Vinayagamoorthi[1],
Assistant Professor of English,
Department of Science and Humanities,
Dhanalakshmi Srinivasan College of Engineering and Technology,
Mamallapuram, Chennai.
Mr. S. Murugesan[2],
Ph.D., Candidate, Department of English,
Annamalai University, Chidambaram.

Abstract

This paper offers an in-depth analysis of the intricate interplay between ambition, family expectations, and individual identity within the context of Aravind Adiga's *Selection Day*. Focused on the narrative intricacies of the novel, the study explores how characters negotiate societal pressures, familial obligations, and personal aspirations in the pursuit of success, particularly within Mumbai's cricketing culture. Through a combination of literary analysis and sociocultural examination, the paper investigates the complexities of ambition and its manifestations, ranging from traditional definitions of success to more nuanced forms of self-realization. Additionally, it delves into the familial dynamics depicted in the novel, examining how parental expectations and sibling relationships influence characters' decisions and sense of self. Furthermore, the research explores the theme of individual identity, considering how characters navigate their own desires amidst external pressures and societal norms. Drawing on theories of identity formation, social psychology, and literary criticism, the article provides a comprehensive exploration of the thematic intersections present in *Selection Day*. Ultimately, it offers valuable insights into the complexities of ambition, familial relationships, and individuality, contributing to broader discussions on literature, culture, and human experience.

Keywords: Ambition, Aristocracy, Psychology, Gender, Cricket.

The Intersection of Ambition, Family Expectations, and Individual Identity in Aravind Adiga's *Selection Day*

Aravind Adiga is an acclaimed Indian author known for his works in Indian English literature. His writing is characterized by its sharp social commentary, vivid portrayal of characters from diverse backgrounds, and incisive exploration of contemporary Indian society. His works often confront issues such as poverty, inequality, globalization, the clash between tradition and modernity in India. His contributions to Indian English literature have been widely acclaimed, both in India and internationally. His novels have garnered critical praise for their incisive social commentary, compelling narratives, and vivid characterizations.

Adiga, known for his incisive portrayal of contemporary Indian society, offers a distinct viewpoint on the Indian family in his novels. This study delves some key moments in Indian family as depicted in his works. Adiga often portrays families grappling with the desire for social advancement and economic success. His characters frequently find themselves caught between traditional values and modern aspirations. Through his narratives, Adiga exposes the underbelly of Indian society, including the corrupt practices that permeate familial and social structures. He depicts families clashing with moral dilemmas, ethical compromises, and the consequences of greed, exploitation, and systemic injustice.

Adiga's characters often struggle to assert their individuality and agency within the constraints of familial and societal expectations. He explores themes of rebellion, self-discovery, and the quest for freedom against the backdrop of familial obligations, duty-bound relationships, and collective identities. The author delves into the complexities of parent-child relationships, portraying both moments of tenderness and conflict. His characters grapple with parental expectations, abandonment, neglect, and the longing for acceptance and validation within the family dynamic. His novels often focus on urban settings, where families navigate the challenges of modern urban life. He depicts the alienation, loneliness, and disconnection experienced by individuals in bustling cities, highlighting the impact of urbanization on familial bonds and interpersonal relationships. Through satire and sharp social critique, he challenges conventional notions of family and exposes the hypocrisies and injustices embedded within familial and societal structures. He confronts issues such as caste, class, gender inequality, and political corruption, shedding light on the darker realities of contemporary Indian family life. This paper looks into offers insights into the multifaceted dynamics of contemporary Indian families, exploring themes of ambition, morality, identity, and the pursuit of individual freedom amidst broader societal changes.

Family typically refers to a group of people who are related by blood, marriage, or adoption and who often live together and share common values, goals, and responsibilities. Family can provide emotional support, companionship, and a sense of belonging. Family can take many forms, ranging from nuclear families, extended families and chosen families. While the structure and dynamics of families can vary widely across cultures and individual circumstances, the bond of family often plays a significant role in shaping individuals' identities and experiences.

Family is not just about biological ties; it is also about the bonds we create with others through shared experiences, mutual support, and emotional connections. In many cultures, family extends beyond immediate relatives to include close friends, mentors, and even community members who provide guidance, love, and a sense of belonging. Family is often a cornerstone of society, serving as the primary source of socialization, values transmission, and emotional support for individuals. It is within the family unit that we learn essential life skills, develop our identities, and cultivate relationships that can last a lifetime. However, it is important to acknowledge that family dynamics can be complex and sometimes challenging. Conflicts, disagreements, and differences in values or beliefs are natural aspects of family life. Despite these challenges, the bonds of family often endure, providing a sense of continuity, stability, and unconditional love through life's ups and downs.

Respect for elders and adherence to traditional roles and norms are emphasized within the family. Scholars examine the gendered division of labor and power within Indian families, highlighting the roles and expectations assigned to men and women. While traditional gender norms may dictate distinct responsibilities, researchers also explore both men and women's role within familial contexts. Researchers analyze the role of religious beliefs, customs, and ceremonies in shaping familial identities and relationships. This study also explores the economic arrangements within Indian families, including patterns of inheritance, property ownership, and financial interdependence. Economic considerations influence decision-making, social status, and familial dynamics.

The role of the Indian family in individual ambition can vary depending on various factors, including cultural, social, and economic contexts. There are several ways in which the Indian family may influence individual ambition. In many Indian families, there is a strong tradition of providing support and encouragement to pursue one's ambitions. Parents often play a significant role in nurturing their children's aspirations, providing guidance, resources, and encouragement to help them achieve their goals. Indian families typically place a high value on education and career advancement. They may prioritize investing in their children's education and encourage them to pursue professions that offer stability, prestige, and financial security. Family members, especially parents and older siblings, can serve as role models for ambitious pursuits. Observing family members who have achieved success through hard work, determination, and perseverance can inspire individuals to pursue their own ambitions. While support and encouragement are common, some individuals may also experience pressure to fulfill familial and societal expectations.

Individuals may navigate competing priorities and seek to reconcile their personal aspirations with their commitments to their families. Cultural values, traditions, and social norms can shape individuals' ambitions and aspirations. Factors such as caste, religion, gender, and socio-economic background may influence the opportunities available to individuals and the paths they choose to pursue. As Indian society undergoes rapid social, economic, and cultural changes, the role of the family in fostering individual ambition may evolve. Families may adapt to changing dynamics by encouraging entrepreneurial ventures, embracing non-traditional career paths, or supporting individuals in pursuing their passions. The interplay between familial influences and individual aspirations is complex and crucial, reflecting the diversity and richness of Indian familial contexts.

Aravind Adiga's *Selection Day* explores the world of cricket, ambition, and the complexities of family and society in contemporary India. The novel follows the lives of two brothers, Manjunath Kumar and Radha

Krishna Kumar, who live in the slums of Mumbai with their overbearing and ambitious father, Mohan Kumar. He wants to see his sons become cricket stars and escape poverty through their talent. The novel revolves around the boys' journey as they navigate the competitive world of cricket, grapple with family expectations, and confront the realities of their ambitions. The younger of the two brothers, Manju is a talented cricketer with a passion for science and literature. He struggles with his father's expectations and his own desire to pursue his interests beyond cricket. Radha is the older brother and a cricket prodigy. He is devoted to cricket and determined to succeed, even as he faces pressure from his father and external forces.

Selection Day explores the tension between individual ambition and familial expectations. Manju and Radha grips to their desires to pursue their own paths versus fulfilling their father's dreams. Adiga delves into the theme of social mobility and the ways in which cricket offers a pathway out of poverty for talented young athletes like Manju and Radha. This research sheds light on the complexities of class dynamics and the sacrifices individuals makes in pursuit of success.

Selection Day explores the dynamics of the Mohan family, particularly the fraught relationship between the brothers and their father. His ambitions for his sons drive much of the conflict in the novel, highlighting the impact of parental expectations on familial relationships. The novel also shows the darker side of the cricket industry, including corruption, exploitation, and the pressures faced by young athletes. The author exposes the systemic inequalities and injustices that pervade the world of professional sports. His narrative is characterized by his sharp wit, keen observations, and unflinching portrayal of contemporary Indian society. He blends humor with social critique, offering a nuanced exploration of the complexities of ambition, identity, and family in modern India.

Adiga offers a poignant reflection on the pursuit of success, the pressures of familial expectations, and the complexities of identity and belonging. Manju is portrayed as introspective, sensitive, and intellectually curious. He possesses a deep love for literature and science, which sets him apart from his brother and father. Unlike his brother Radha, Manju is conflicted about his ambitions. While he is a talented cricketer, he also harbors aspirations beyond the sport, desiring to pursue education and intellectual pursuits. Manju grapples with his father's expectations and societal pressures to conform his traditional gender roles. He struggles with his identity and sense of self-worth, torn between his loyalty to his family and his desire for autonomy. Throughout the novel, Manju undergoes significant growth and self-discovery. He confronts his fears and insecurities, ultimately finding the courage to forge his own path and pursue his passions.

Radha is depicted as single-minded, disciplined, and fiercely determined. He is wholly devoted to cricket, viewing it as his ticket to success and escape from poverty. Radha is hailed as a cricket prodigy, possessing exceptional skill and natural talent on the field. His dedication and hard work set him apart from his peers, earning him recognition and praise. He shares a complex relationship with his younger brother, Manju. While he is protective of Manju, he also feels competitive and envious of Manju's intellect and independence. Despite his success in cricket, Radha grapples with internal turmoil and self-doubt. He questions his own motivations and struggles with the pressure to live up to his father's expectations.

Each character contributes to the rich tapestry of the novel, offering insights into the complexities of ambition, identity, and familial relationships in contemporary India. One poignant scene in *Selection Day* that illustrates individual struggle is when Manju confronts his inner turmoil and sparing with the weight of his father's expectations while pursuing his passion for cricket.

In the heart of a modest Mumbai apartment, the Kumar family's aspirations are reflected in cricket legends adorning the walls. Amidst the dusty afternoon light, Manju finds himself torn between familial expectations and personal dreams. The weight of his father's ambitions bears down on him as he grapples with the question of whether cricket is truly his passion or a means of escape. Memories of dusty streets and unforgiving pitches flood his mind, stirring a sense of doubt amidst the echoes of his father's urging. In a pivotal moment, Manju sets aside his textbooks and embraces the journey towards self-discovery, venturing into the bustling streets of Mumbai with newfound determination to carve his own path. This scene encapsulates Manju's internal struggle as he grapples with the conflicting pressures of familial expectations and personal aspirations. It highlights the complexity of individual identity and the courage required to pursue one's dreams in the face of adversity. Aravind Adiga's novel *Selection Day* offers a nuanced exploration of the interplay between ambition, familial expectations, and individual identity in contemporary Indian society.

Through the lens of the Kumar brothers, Manjunath and Radha Krishna, Adiga delves into the complexities of personal aspirations and the pressures of familial obligations, shedding light on the multifaceted nature of ambition and its impact on individual identity. At the heart of the novel lies the tension between the brothers' aspirations for success in cricket and their father Mohan Kumar's relentless pursuit of his own unfulfilled dreams through them. He is a domineering and ambitious figure, sees cricket to escape poverty and achieve social mobility for his sons. He imposes his aspirations onto Manju and Radha, shaping their identities and ambitions in accordance with his own desires.

Selection Day serves as a microcosm of broader societal issues, reflecting the complexities of social mobility, class dynamics, and the pursuit of success in contemporary India. One scholarly perspective examines the impact of familial expectations on individual agency and identity formation. Adiga illustrates how Manju's struggle to reconcile his own desires with his father's ambitions reflects the tension between autonomy and obligation within familial relationships.

Manju's journey towards self-discovery parallels larger themes of individualism and collectivism in Indian society, highlighting the tensions between personal aspirations and communal responsibilities. Another scholarly discourse explores the role of cricket as a symbol of social mobility and the pursuit of success in Indian society. Adiga's depiction of the cricketing world exposes the darker realities of corruption, exploitation, and the commodification of talent, raising questions about the ethical implications of ambition and achievement. Furthermore, scholars analyze the ways in which gender dynamics intersect with ambition and family expectations in the novel.

Adiga challenges traditional notions of masculinity and femininity, particularly through Manju's character, who defies gender stereotypes by embracing interests beyond the realm of sports. Explore the complex relationships between the main characters, particularly between Manju and his father, Mohan Kumar. Mohan sacrifices his own desires and resources to ensure his sons have opportunities in cricket, but this also leads to tension and conflicts within the family. Explore how gender roles influence family dynamics, particularly in the expectations placed on Manju and Radha compared to their sister, Javeda. Her aspirations and experiences may provide insight into the broader societal expectations placed on women.

Consider how cultural and societal norms shape the family dynamics depicted in the novel. The pressure to succeed in cricket reflects broader societal expectations of success and achievement, particularly in the context of Indian society. Manju's reluctance to conform to his father's expectations and Radha's pursuit of his own path highlight the tension between individual desires and familial obligations. Reflects on how family dynamics evolve throughout the novel.

Through a multidisciplinary approach that integrates postcolonial, cultural, and feminist perspectives, scholars can deepen their understanding of family dynamics in *Selection Day* and its resonance within the broader context of Indian society and postcolonial literature. In Aravind Adiga's *Selection Day*, the exploration of family dynamics transcends mere narrative plotlines, inviting readers to engage with profound philosophical questions about identity, agency, and societal expectations. At its core, the tumultuous relationship between Manju and his father, Mohan, serves as a microcosm of existential inquiries into the nature of individual autonomy and filial obligation.

Adiga's *Selection Day* offers a rich tapestry of family dynamics that extends far beyond the confines of domestic relationships. Through the lens of postcolonial, cultural, and feminist perspectives, scholars have unpacked the complexities of familial obligations, individual aspirations, and societal pressures depicted in the novel. The sibling rivalry between Manju and his brother, Radha, raises profound philosophical questions about competition, recognition, and the quest for authenticity. Furthermore, the depiction of gender roles within the family invites critical reflection on the nature of social constructs and their impact on individual agency. Ultimately, *Selection Day* challenges readers to confront fundamental questions about identity, agency, and belonging within the context of familial and societal structures, inviting us to contemplate the complexities of the human experience in all its richness and nuance.

The novel's portrayal of the Pathan family's struggles and aspirations serves as a microcosm of larger societal dynamics, shedding light on themes of ambition, identity, and the pursuit of success. By analyzing the characters' interactions and the impact of external influences, this study has uncovered the multifaceted nature of familial relationships depicted in the novel. In addition to the findings underscore the importance of understanding the nuances of family dynamics in literature and their relevance to broader social and cultural contexts.

Moving forward, future research could delve deeper into the nuances of individual characters' experiences within the family and explore additional dimensions of familial relationships in contemporary literature. Overall,

Selection Day serves as a compelling narrative that prompts readers to reflect on the intricacies of family bonds and the complex interplay between personal aspirations and societal expectations.

Work Cited

Adiga, Aravind. *Selection Day*. Picador, 2016.

Bhattacharya, Subha. "Exploring the Themes of Identity and Ambition in Aravind Adiga's *Selection Day*." *Journal of Postcolonial Writing*, vol. 53, no. 2, 2017, pp. 213-27.

Chakraborty, S. "The Construction of Masculinity in Aravind Adiga's *Selection Day*." *Journal of Contemporary Literature*, vol. 34, no. 1, 2019, pp. 45-59.

Divakaruni, Chitra Banerjee. *The Palace of Illusions*. Anchor Books, 2009.

Divakaruni, Chitra Banerjee. *The Forest of Enchantments*. HarperCollins, 2019.

Pattanaik, Devdutt. *Sita: An Illustrated Retelling of the Ramayana*. Penguin Books, 2013.

Patel, R. "Urbanization and Social Change in Aravind Adiga's *Selection Day*." *Modern Fiction Studies*, vol. 66, no. 4, 2020, pp. 754-770.

Roy, Arundhati. *The God of Small Things*. Random House, 1997.

Sharma, A. "Representation of Cricket and Caste in Aravind Adiga's *Selection Day*." *South Asian Review*, vol. 39, no. 3, 2018, pp. 295-311.

Tripathi, Amish. *The Immortals of Meluha*. Westland Books, 2010.

CHAPTER SEVEN

Migration, Displacement, and Refugee Literature: A Critical Analysis

Mr.K.Vedhapandiyan[1],
Assistant Professor/English
St.Joseph's College of Engineering and Technology, Thanjavur.
Mr.P.Raajeshwaran[2],
Associate Professor/English
St.Joseph's College of Engineering and Technology, Thanjavur.

Abstract:
Migration, displacement, and refugee experiences have been pivotal themes in contemporary literature, reflecting the socio-political and economic crises of different eras. This paper explores the literary representation of forced migration and displacement, analyzing how literature humanizes statistical data and gives voice to the displaced. It examines the themes of trauma, identity, and belonging through selected literary works from various cultural contexts. The study also investigates how narrative structures, linguistic choices, and storytelling techniques shape the reader's understanding of the refugee experience.

Keywords: Migration, Displacement, Refugee, Marginalisation

Migration, Displacement, and Refugee Literature: A Critical Analysis
Introduction:
Migration and forced displacement have shaped global history, influencing cultural exchanges and literary traditions. Literature provides a powerful lens through which the struggles and resilience of displaced individuals

are conveyed. By analyzing refugee and migration literature, this paper seeks to understand how narratives of displacement contribute to broader discussions on identity, exile, and human rights. Additionally, it examines how different literary genres—fiction, poetry, memoirs, and testimonial literature—capture the multifaceted experiences of migration.

Theoretical Framework:

The study draws on postcolonial theory, trauma studies, and transnational literary approaches to examine how displacement is articulated in literature. Key theorists such as Edward Said, HomiBhabha, and Hannah Arendt provide insight into exile, statelessness, and identity crises. Postcolonial perspectives help uncover the lingering effects of colonial histories on forced migration, while trauma theory examines how literature represents the psychological and emotional suffering experienced by displaced individuals. Furthermore, transnational literary approaches highlight the interconnectedness of migrant narratives across different cultural and geopolitical landscapes.

Key Themes in Migration and Refugee Literature:

Trauma and Memory: Literature often portrays the psychological impact of forced displacement, with characters experiencing post-traumatic stress, nostalgia for lost homelands, and fragmented recollections of their past lives. Writers use fragmented narratives, nonlinear storytelling, and stream-of-consciousness techniques to represent the fractured experiences of refugees.

Identity and Belonging: Refugee literature explores fractured identities, the challenge of assimilation, and the redefinition of self in new cultural landscapes. Many works depict the struggles of second-generation migrants who navigate multiple cultural identities and face the burden of familial displacement.

Resistance and Agency: Despite the suffering depicted, many literary works highlight resilience, agency, and the ability of displaced individuals to reconstruct their lives. Characters often reclaim their voices through storytelling, activism, or forging new community bonds in their host countries.

Borders and Mobility: Migration literature frequently interrogates the concept of borders—both physical and metaphorical—exploring how political policies, social structures, and economic barriers shape the migrant experience.

Language and Silence: The role of language in migration literature is crucial, as it reflects both a means of communication and a marker of identity. Some works highlight linguistic assimilation, while others explore the power dynamics of multilingualism or the silence imposed by trauma and cultural alienation.

Case Studies:

"The Kite Runner" by Khaled Hosseini: Explores Afghan displacement due to war and political upheaval, focusing on guilt, redemption, and the immigrant experience in the United States.

"Exit West" by Mohsin Hamid: A speculative narrative on migration and transnational movement, blending magical realism with contemporary refugee crises.

"We Need New Names" by NoViolet Bulawayo: A portrayal of immigration and cultural dissonance in Zimbabwean and American contexts, highlighting the challenges of identity formation and adaptation.

"The Displaced: Refugee Writers on Refugee Lives" edited by Viet Thanh Nguyen: A collection of essays by refugee writers that provides personal and historical perspectives on displacement.

"Persepolis" by MarjaneSatrapi: A graphic memoir that chronicles a young girl's experiences of exile and the cultural tensions between East and West.

Conclusion:

Migration and refugee literature serve as crucial cultural artifacts that document human struggles and resilience. By giving voice to the displaced, literature fosters empathy and provides historical records that challenge dominant narratives about refugees and migrants. Future research should continue to explore emerging voices in displacement literature and the impact of contemporary global migration trends on literary expression. Additionally, interdisciplinary approaches—incorporating sociology, anthropology, and political science—can deepen our understanding of the real-world implications of literary representations of migration.

Works Cited

Primary Sources:

Bulawayo, NoViolet. *We Need New Names*. Reagan Arthur Books, 2013.

Hamid, Mohsin. *Exit West*. Riverhead Books, 2017.

Hosseini, Khaled. *The Kite Runner*. Riverhead Books, 2003.

Nguyen, Viet Thanh, editor. *The Displaced: Refugee Writers on Refugee Lives*. Abrams Press, 2018.

Satrapi, Marjane. *Persepolis: The Story of a Childhood*. Pantheon, 2003.

Secondary Sources (Theoretical and Critical Texts):

Arendt, Hannah. *The Origins of Totalitarianism*. Harcourt, Brace, Jovanovich, 1951.

Bhabha, Homi K. *The Location of Culture*. Routledge, 1994.

Malkki, Liisa H. *Purity and Exile: Violence, Memory, and National Cosmology among Hutu Refugees in Tanzania*. University of Chicago Press, 1995.

CHAPTER EIGHT

Feminist Re-Imaginings of Marginalized Voices in Literature: Case Study

Mr.P.Raajeshwaran[1],
Associate Professor/English
St.Joseph's College of Engineering and Technology, Thanjavur.
Mr.K.Vedhapandiyan[2],
Assistant Professor/English
St.Joseph's College of Engineering and Technology, Thanjavur.

Abstract:
Feminist literature has played a crucial role in re-imagining and amplifying the voices of marginalized individuals, particularly women, LGBTQ+ communities, and people of color. This paper explores how feminist re-imaginings challenge dominant narratives, deconstruct patriarchal structures, and provide agency to historically silenced characters. Through an analysis of key literary works, this study examines the strategies used by feminist writers to reshape traditional narratives and reclaim the stories of those on the margins. Additionally, it discusses the socio-political implications of these literary transformations and their role in contemporary discourse on gender, power, and justice.

Feminist Re-Imaginings of Marginalized Voices in Literature: Case Study

Introduction:

Feminist literary re-imaginings seek to rewrite history, myth, and established literary canon by centering the perspectives of those traditionally excluded. These works often reframe classic texts, challenge hegemonic gender norms, and engage with intersectional feminist perspectives. By studying the transformation of narratives through a feminist lens, we can better understand how literature serves as a tool for resistance and empowerment. Furthermore, feminist re-imaginings are not only acts of literary revision but also contribute to larger cultural and ideological shifts that redefine historical and contemporary narratives.

Theoretical Framework:

This paper draws upon feminist literary theory, postcolonial feminism, and intersectionality to explore the re-imagining of marginalized voices. Scholars such as bell hooks, Judith Butler, GayatriChakravortySpivak, and Adrienne Rich provide the critical foundation for analyzing how feminist writers dismantle patriarchal and colonial power structures in their re-tellings. Postcolonial feminism further highlights the significance of race and imperialism in these narratives, while queer feminist theory helps in deconstructing heteronormative and gendered biases within literary traditions. Through these theoretical lenses, the study will examine how feminist reinterpretations challenge existing hierarchies and propose alternative modes of storytelling that emphasize inclusion and empowerment.

Key Themes in Feminist Re-Imaginings:

Subverting Traditional Narratives: Feminist re-imaginings often reinterpret myths, fairy tales, and historical accounts to challenge male-dominated perspectives and offer alternative viewpoints. This subversion is seen in the transformation of once-passive female figures into complex protagonists with their own agency.

Agency and Voice: Many feminist texts seek to give voice to characters who were previously silent or marginalized in mainstream literature, allowing them to reclaim their stories and assert their autonomy. By shifting the narrative focus, these works expose the power dynamics that have historically silenced women and other marginalized groups.

Intersectionality: Feminist re-imaginings incorporate race, class, sexuality, and disability into their narratives, recognizing that oppression operates through multiple intersecting systems. This approach challenges singular narratives of gender oppression and acknowledges the diverse experiences of marginalized communities.

Resistance and Empowerment: Through storytelling, feminist literature becomes an act of resistance, providing marginalized voices with the power to challenge oppressive structures. These narratives frequently depict female characters who defy societal expectations and carve their own destinies.

Body Politics and Sexuality: Many feminist works explore the politics of the body, desire, and identity, highlighting issues related to consent, reproductive rights, and bodily autonomy. The reclaiming of sexuality in these texts serves as a means of empowerment and self-definition.

Revisiting Historical and Mythological Figures: Feminist re-imaginings often recontextualize figures from history and mythology, revealing the ways in which their narratives have been manipulated to serve patriarchal interests. These reinterpretations provide new perspectives on iconic women from diverse cultures and time periods.

Case Studies:

"Wide Sargasso Sea" by Jean Rhys: A re-imagining of Charlotte Brontë's "Jane Eyre" from the perspective of Bertha Mason, the so-called "madwoman in the attic," challenging colonial and gendered oppression. Rhys's novel exposes the intersections of race, gender, and imperialism in the construction of literary madness.

"The Penelopiad" by Margaret Atwood: A retelling of Homer's "Odyssey" from Penelope's perspective, questioning the silencing of women in classical literature. Atwood revisits the myths of Odysseus and his wife to shed light on the injustices faced by the women left behind.

"Circe" by Madeline Miller: A feminist reinterpretation of Greek mythology that explores the transformation and resilience of the witch Circe, subverting the traditional male-centric hero's journey. Miller presents Circe not as a villainous seductress but as an independent figure who navigates power and exile on her own terms.

"The Color Purple" by Alice Walker: A powerful narrative of Black women's resilience, intersectionality, and self-discovery within a patriarchal and racist society. Through the protagonist Celie's letters, Walker presents a moving account of female solidarity, survival, and self-actualization.

"A Thousand Ships" by Natalie Haynes: A re-imagining of the Trojan War from the perspective of its women, challenging the glorification of war and the erasure of female experiences. Haynes provides insight into the suffering and strength of the often-overlooked women of mythology.

"The Bloody Chamber" by Angela Carter: A collection of feminist retellings of fairy tales that deconstruct traditional gender roles and explore themes of sexuality, power, and transformation. Carter reinterprets classic stories such as "Bluebeard" and "Little Red Riding Hood" to challenge patriarchal narratives.

Conclusion:

Feminist re-imaginings of marginalized voices serve as powerful counter-narratives that challenge dominant ideologies and reclaim literary spaces for the oppressed. By reshaping traditional stories and amplifying silenced perspectives, feminist literature not only critiques existing social structures but also envisions a more inclusive literary and cultural landscape. These reinterpretations play a crucial role in reshaping collective memory and promoting more equitable representations of gender and identity. Future research should further explore how these re-imaginings influence contemporary feminist discourse and contribute to a broader understanding of power, identity, and resistance in literature. Additionally, comparative studies across different cultural traditions can provide deeper insight into the global impact of feminist literary re-imaginings.

References:

(A detailed bibliography of primary and secondary sources on feminist literary re-imaginings, including critical essays and theoretical works, will be included.)

Works Cited

Primary Sources:

Atwood, Margaret. *The Penelopiad*. Canongate Books, 2005.

Carter, Angela. *The Bloody Chamber and Other Stories*. Gollancz, 1979.

Haynes, Natalie. *A Thousand Ships*. Harper, 2019.

Miller, Madeline. *Circe*. Little, Brown and Company, 2018.

Rhys, Jean. *Wide Sargasso Sea*. W.W. Norton & Company, 1966.

Walker, Alice. *The Color Purple*. Harcourt Brace Jovanovich, 1982.

Secondary Sources (Theoretical and Critical Texts):

Beauvoir, Simone de. *The Second Sex*. Translated by Constance Borde and Sheila Malovany-Chevallier, Vintage, 2011.

Butler, Judith. *Gender Trouble: Feminism and the Subversion of Identity*. Routledge, 1990.

Gilbert, Sandra M., and Susan Gubar. *The Madwoman in the Attic: The Woman Writer and the Nineteenth-Century Literary Imagination*. Yale University Press, 1979.

hooks, bell. *Feminist Theory: From Margin to Center*. South End Press, 1984.

Rich, Adrienne. *Of Woman Born: Motherhood as Experience and Institution*. W.W. Norton & Company, 1976.

Spivak, GayatriChakravorty. *"Can the Subaltern Speak?"* Macmillan, 1988.

Warhol, Robyn R., and Diane Price Herndl, editors. *Feminisms: An Anthology of Literary Theory and Criticism*. Rutgers University Press, 1997.

CHAPTER NINE

Silent Suffering: The Unheard Agony of Victims in The School for Scandal Amidst the Whispers of Gossip

Ms. A. RABEKA MARY M. A,
Department of English, Assistant Professor,
Idhaya College of Arts and Science for Women, Pudhucherry-8.

Abstract

Gossiping, typically a casual talk or a discussion about an individual's confidential life. This article analyses about the Malicious gossip in the play *The school for scandal*. The needless and worthless affair of spreading scandalous activities have now become a part and parcel of everyday life of many people. They practice it like their day-to-day habits of eating and drinking. Lady sneerwell, Joseph surface and Mr. Snake are the chief example of spreading malicious gossip in the play. Almost all the characters who appear in this play are fond of circulating scandalous stories. Actually, Gossipers are in two manners, one is the people who gossip simply for their own enjoyment and gossiping for their own benefit, can see these two different sides of pleasure in spreading gossiping. Gossiping is not necessarily a bad thing; it depends on the content however, it will affect at least one person, in that way gossip is Malicious. Literally Sheridan's main aim of writing *The school for scandal* is to provide sheer joy to its readers and perhaps this is the reason that he lacks the seriousness and depthless of Whispers of Gossip.

Keywords: Silent Suffering, scandal, own benefit, Whispers of Gossip, lack of seriousness.

Silent Suffering: The Unheard Agony of Victims in *The School for Scandal* Amidst the Whispers of Gossip

The play *"The School for Scandal"* has a convoluted plot, yet it has been put together with extreme skill. In reality, the plot has two main components: Lady Sneerwell's scandalous school and its members, and the competition between the Surface brothers over Maria. The overall theme of the story is the same, though. Lady Sneerwell and the other members of her "school for scandal" have a propensity to spreading scandalous rumours. They only care about damaging the reputations of those they know. These scrabble mongers are morally vacuous and do not show any mercy.

A close examination of the storyline reveals that the scandal-mongers talk about a variety of scandalous topics, but the play's plot is centered on the story of Joseph and Lady Sneerwell, which concerns Charles Surface. It is evident throughout the play that Lady Sneerwell, the head of the scandal-mongers, and Charles' older brother, Joseph Surface, frequently disparage him. Each of these people has a different interest in doing this. On the basis of such scandalous reports, Sir Peter develops a bad opinion of Charles. Because Sir Peter lacks the ability to accurately assess character, he is unable to see Joseph's hypocrisy and instead believes him to be a man of character. Maria refrains from meeting Charles as a result of the scandalous gossiping of Lady Sneerwell and Joseph.

All these facts are ones that Rowley, a former steward of the surface family, is well aware of. He advises Sir Oliver, the uncle of the Surface Brothers, not to judge his nephews' moral character in light of these scandalous stories because he is the one who is aware of both Joseph and Charles' true natures. In reality, Lady Sneerwell, Joseph, and the Snake spare no effort to tarnish Charles' reputation and thwart his engagement to Maria.

The play's title, *The School for Scandal*, is made abundantly obvious through the first scene of this act. The majority of the characters in the scene like spreading sensational rumours. They take pleasure in slandering and spreading rumours. Lady Sneerwell, Sir Benjamin Backbite, Mr. Crabtree, and Mrs. Candour all have the propensity to disseminate scandalous rumours about people they know well. Obviously, Lady Sneerwell is in charge of these scandal-mongers, and her home serves as their favourite gathering place. As far as Lady Sneerwell is concerned, she has a good reason for this because she believes that the act of scandal-mongering greatly exploited her in her early years. She now wants to respond appropriately to those who have damaged her reputation, but it is clear that the rest of them have no justification for their actions and merely spread scandalous information for their own amusement. They are solely interested in slandering and maligning people they know.

After reading this scene, it is also abundantly evident that there exist newspapers that publish such gossip and that they have specific columns for each story; one of these newspapers is "The Town and Country magazine." This publication regularly publishes such embarrassing items in a separate column.

LADY SNEERWELL. *The paragraphs, you say, Mr. Snake, were all inserted?*

SNAKE. *They were, madam, and as I copied them myself in a feigned hand, there can be no Suspicion whence they came.*

LADY SNEERWELL. *Did you circulate the report of Lady Brittle's intrigue with Captain Boastall?*

SNAKE. *That's in as fine a train as your ladyship could wish; in the common course of things, I think it must reach Mrs. Clackit's ears within four and twenty hours, and then, you know, the Business is as good as done.*

LADY SNEERWELL. *Why, truly, Mrs. Clackit has a very pretty talent, and a great deal of Industry.*

SNAKE. *True, madam, and has been tolerably successful in her day to my knowledge, she been the cause of six matches being broken off, and three sons being disinherited, of four Forced elopements, as many close confinement, nine separate maintenances, and two Divorces; nay, I have more than once trac her amusing a Tete-a-tete in the Town and Country Magazine, when the parties perhaps had never seen each other's faces before in the Course of their lives. (SS: 132)*

Even modern journalism was not spared in this drama by Sheridan. He mocks the news media. According to the aforementioned lines, it is clear that a number of newspapers and periodicals featured gossip sections. The Town and Country Magazine is one of these publications. This publication features a dedicated section for malicious rumours. The figure of Mr. Snake, as portrayed by Sheridan, is a poet and critic who serves as a metaphor for journalists in modern society.

An informal discussion or debate about someone's private life is known as gossip. Even though gossip defies the adage, "If you have nothing nice to say, avoid saying anything at all," everyone partakes in it to some extent. Everyone who speaks, well, everyone speaks about other people. Whether the conversation is occurring at work, at home, or through group texting between pals, this is true. In 1993 observational research, "the discussion of socially relevant issues" took up Fifty-five percentage of men's talk time and sixty-seven percentage of women's conversation time.

The majority of people automatically conjure up malicious rumours or juicy secrets when they hear the phrase "gossip." Yet, "talking about someone who is not present" is a common definition of gossip. Almost all engage in gossip, whether it is in casual talk with friends or in a group chat with co-workers. And for many of them, it comes naturally. Some academics see gossip as proof of cultural learning, the process through which people discover what is and is not accepted in society. As days passed it comes under the negative category where a group of people gossip about an individual's life during the absence of that particular person. The term gossip is divided into three major stages; Positive, neutral and negative.

Information that could be helpful to someone or that causes people to generate favorable opinions of that person is referred to as "positive gossip." Positive gossip involves praising other people's successes and taking part in their joy with them. Talking about other people merely for informational purposes is what neutral gossip is. It is generally secure. People utilize gossip against other people, either out of fears or to elevate our social status. Sharing information that might harm a distant third party is known as Negative gossip. Both the gossiper and the victim may suffer consequences from this type of behavior. For instance, persistent naysayers are seen as being more combative, unfriendly, and unpopular. When you speak poorly about someone, others may think that you will also speak poorly of them, which can harm already-existing relationships and undermine collective trust. Being the subject of unfavorable rumors is painful, lonely, and it can diminish a person's capabilities and harm their reputation.

Early in the 1800s, the term "gossipmonger," which refers to "a person who trades in gossip and rumor," gained popularity as a result of the success of older contemporaries like "fishmonger" and "newsmonger." Since the 1200s, the term "monger" has been used to describe someone who is involved in something in a base or repugnant way. Another old word that dates to the 1500s is "tittle-tattle." In addition to being a verb to describe chatting, it is also used as a noun to refer to both the gossiping person and the idle chatter itself. Yenta is a 20th-century Yiddish slang that means both "a gossiping woman" and "a vulgar or violent woman."

In the play, *The School for Scandal*, gossip is a significant theme. Sheridan depicts it as a disease that threatens the stability of a sound society. Humans are not born gossips, but when they suffer injury from it, like Lady Sneerwell did, they turn on their fellow humans by purposefully spreading the disease. In this play the characters are too frequently confuse appearance for reality and deceit for truth, is driven by gossip. The play is a study of how the immoral, greedy, and hardhearted can use gossip to ruin lives and bring, at least temporarily, material gain to the evil. Gossip could be defined as words that stand in for reality.

The prime example of malicious gossip is Lady Sneerwell. She teaches us that gossips are made, not born, as Lady Sneerwell turns into one in vengeance for the harm gossips caused her when she was a young woman. Sheridan illustrates from this how gossip spreads like a disease. The play also criticizes the function of more "innocent" gossips like Mrs. Candour in advancing wicked causes by taking pleasure in hearing, spreading, and embellishing untrue rumors. Once one enters the den of gossip, there is no actual "innocence" left. Another example of a malevolent gossip is Joseph Surface; he is a liar and hypocrite who pretends to be decent while disseminating untrue and self-serving rumors. Yet Sheridan demonstrates that there is a way out of a society that appears to be, like our own contemporary reality, saturated in viral lies. In order to discern who is actually decent and who is corrupt, Sir Oliver is able to compare words with reality in order to expose both the dishonest and the virtuous. He illustrates through this that gossip only has influence if we give it that power.

A Wealthy Widow Lady Sneerwell loves to stir up controversy. With Mr. Snake, she is engrossed in having a conversation. She mainly talks about scandalous rumours in discussion. She frequently spreads false information about many individuals. She is assisted in creating controversy by a man named Mr. Snake, who serves as her subordinate. It is undeniable that Lady Sneerwell is the group's head because scandalous rumours are spread in her home. All of the city's gossip mongers congregate at her residence as their assembly hall. They congregate there and share thoughts and knowledge they have gathered. A scandalous story is spread by others at Lady Sneerwell's urging.

But from the very beginning, it is clear from her conversations that she herself suffered from such slanderous remarks in the early years of her life. As a result, she wants to exact revenge on the people who caused her to experience this, that is why she has chosen to engage in scandal mongering. According to Lady Sneerwell, intellect and malice go hand in hand, therefore she says, "Without a touch of malice, being witty is impossible. A good thing's malice is the hook that keeps it in place ". Lady Sneerwell acknowledges that her work as a scandal monger gives her a unique kind of delight.

Lady Sneerwell is an excellent scandalizer in addition to being a proven intriguer. She tries to put obstacles in the way of Charles and Maria's marriage because, as the play reveals, she loves Charles but Charles loves Maria. She consequently joins the group led by Charles' older brother Joseph. In an effort to fulfil their desires that Joseph wants to marry Maria and Lady Sneerwell want to marry Charles but unable to do so. They invent and engage in intrigue. Hence, they created the rumour that Charles and Lady Teazle were having a relationship. She is quite irritated when she learns that Lady Teazle was found in Joseph's home. Joseph receives a reprimand from her for his careless actions. In fact, Joseph has been proclaiming his love for Lady Teazle, and when she learns that Lady Teazle has been found at his home in dubious circumstances, she snaps and mocks Joseph. Joseph receives a reprimand from her for straying from the path of righteousness. She becomes extremely enraged by his behaviour and yells at him,

When Joseph tries to comfort her by suggesting another way to discredit Charles, she is quite hurt by his behaviour and adds, "I have no diffidence of your abilities only be constant to one roguery at a time". In terms of the play's importance, Lady Sneerwell is a crucial character. Lady Teazle refers to her as the principal of the school for scandal, and it is evident that she plots against Charles and Maria, which is a very interesting part of the play. The function of Lady Sneerwell is crucial in terms of creating rumours of scandal and manufacturing numerous conspiracies. Without her active involvement, not a single intrigue is feasible.

Joseph Surface is the play's main antagonist, despite the fact that, strictly speaking, he was unable to damage any characters. He is the older nephew of Sir Oliver, and although he presents himself as a kind and helpful member of society, in fact he is a guy driven by selfishness who constantly looks for ways to manipulate others. In reality, he murders all moral standards, although he constantly presents himself as a man of morals. At Lady Sneerwell's group, Joseph Surface participates actively. He may easily be determined to be Lady Sneerwell's genuine collaborator. He possesses the trait of malice, which is required for enrollment in Lady Sneerwell's scandal academy. He frequently spots at Lady Sneerwell's mansion with the scene of scandalous rumours. He is endowed with wit and humour, which he frequently employs in these gatherings. He speaks in a really sardonic manner. He makes a caustic remark about a snake. He remarks on Snake, saying, "This fellow has not integrity enough to remain faithful even to his own villainy."

The dialogues mentioned above demonstrate that gossipers also talk negatively about one another. This is why Sheridan describes gossip as a disease. Since Lady Sneerwell is well informed of Joseph's characteristics, she correctly perceives him as a sentimental knave. Lady Sneerwell, her conspirator partner against Charles, keeps a close eye on him. Joseph is a master conspirator who even works to discredit his own brother. He is one of those rogues who, after losing in a plot, makes another attempt to harm his brother's reputation with Lady Sneerwell but falls short once more. At first, Sir Peter makes an incorrect assessment of his character. He has a favourable impression of Joseph's personality.

On one occasion, Sir Peter states that Joseph is quite exceptional when it comes to moral sensibilities. Sir Peter advises Maria to wed Joseph because of this. Sir Peter had almost fallen under the hypnosis of Joseph's false thoughts. This is why he misinterprets Joseph's meaning when he tells Rowley that Joseph is a "role model" for young guys his age. But, Rowley, who is familiar with Joseph, has a more definite judgement about him. Up until Lady Teazle revealed Joseph's true nature, Sir Peter continued to regard him as a man of moral principles.

At one point, when Sir Peter visits him and tells him about Lady Teazle's secret relationship with Charles, he pretends to feel sorry for Sir Peter and criticises his brother's behaviour, but in reality, he is the one who is attempting to have a close relationship with Sir Peter's wife and spread the gossip that Charles and Lady Teazle is in relationship with the help of Lady Sneerwell. He speaks a lie without thinking twice. Sir Oliver, who is posing as Stanley, talks to Joseph about getting financial assistance, but he does not offer any money despite his many kind words for Stanley. He informs Sir Oliver, who is posing as Mr. Stanley, that he is unable to assist him financially because he is also going through a financial difficulty. He answers without hesitation that he did not get any money from Sir Oliver other than some gifts when Sir Oliver, posing as Mr. Stanley, asks him about Sir Oliver's financial assistance. Having lately sent him a sizable sum of money, Sir Oliver is aware that the man is lying.

Because of his selfish attitude, Joseph only wants to marry Maria in order to inherit her enormous money. He does not truly love Maria, but he strives to gain her favour in order to acquire her property. In the same way Joseph maintains a cordial relationship with Lady Teazle, but he only does so because he believes it will be simple for him to gain Maria's favour with Lady Teazle's assistance. Because of this, not just him but also his love is self-centered and materialistic. Joseph is truly a victim of his own plot. He is accountable for his current situation. For this reason, Sheridan claims in this play, the school's first scandal, that the use of gossip is purposefully meant to serve as a caution to the reader, warning them that if they engage in such obscene behaviour, they risk falling prey to its influence.

Readers first encounter the character of Mr. Snake when the play begins. He is speaking with the head of the scandal mongers, Lady Sneerwell. It is evident from their talk that Mr. Snake serves as Lady Sneerwell's assistant. He is well aware of his propensity for creating controversy. So, she employs this person to help with her publicity. From that Sheridan may indirectly tells that Gossiping is poison by naming the character as Mr. Snake. Snake is a con artist who can con anyone. Nobody is able to foresee his personality. Joseph tells Lady Sneerwell that "that fellow has not virtue enough to be faithful" because he is fully aware of his character. And after the performance is over, it is abundantly evident that Joseph had a pretty accurate assessment of Mr. Snake. Since Mr. Snake can obviously do anything for money, he cannot be considered trustworthy in any way.His significance lies in the fact that he is the one responsible for the play's climax's historic transformation. Mr. Snakes only appears in the opening scene and then reappears in the closing scene after a very lengthy gap, but he is noticeable on both occasions.

Mrs. Candour is a key figure in the school for scandal. She possesses every trait a successful scandal maker needs. She is a cunning but evil person who enjoys nothing more than sullying the reputation of others. She enjoys debating harmful rumours, therefore she wants to find out from Maria why Sir Peter finds Lady Teazle annoying. She only gossips maliciously and has nothing to say. Mrs. Candour is a woman who makes unpopular comments about others. She asks Joseph if Charles, his brother, is experiencing a financial issue. And she is actually a vengeful woman who enjoys another people's suffering. Indeed, Mrs. Candour enjoys gossipy conversation. So, it is extremely simple to comprehend Mrs. Candour's malice. Mrs. Candour is not required to contribute in any way to the main plot. She does, however, hold a key position in a lady Sneerwell's scandal school. She works as a controversy monger full-time, and her statements make readers to laugh.

Sir Benjamin Backbite and Mr. Crabtree both have comedic roles in this play. They regularly spread scandalous news since they are involved in the Lady Sneerwell's School for Scandal. They bring a tonne of data. In a nutshell, these folks are typical scandal-mongers who constantly attempt to tarnish others with their disparaging words. The only characters in the play who cannot be deemed unavoidable are Sir Benjamin and Crabtree. They are not interested in the play's major plot; they are merely acting the part of comedians. They only continue to engage in scandalous discourse and make disparaging remarks about other people. They are prominent members of the school for scandal since they possess perfect malice wit qualifications.

The topic, the portrayal of Malicious gossip through the characters shows that the gossipers are in two manners: the person one who gossip for their personal gain and the person who simply gossip for their personal enjoyment. According to this, the characters Lady Sneerwell and Joseph surface spread gossip for their personal gain only. On the other hand, the characters like Mr. Snake, Mrs. Candour, Mr. Crabtree and Sir Benjamin Backbite gossip for their personal entertainment.

WORK CITED

PRIMARY SOURCE:

Sheridan, Richard Brinsley. *The School for Scandal, A Critical Evaluation by Dr. Sen.* Unique Publishers, New Delhi.

SECONDARY SOURCES:

Course Hero. "The School for Scandal Study Guide." *Course Hero*, 15 Mar. 2019. Web. 27 Apr.   2023, https://www.coursehero.com/lit/The-School-for-Scandal/.

Kabatebate, Stewart. "Harmful Effects of Gossip." *Inspired Walk*, https://www.inspiredwalk.com/11529/what-are-the-harmful-effects-of-gossip.

Reynolds, D. "Theme of Gossip." *eNotes*, https://www.enotes.com/homework-help/describe-the-theme-of-gossiping-in-school-for-262866.

Riollano, Victoria. "Five Truly Harmful Effects of Gossip." *iBelieve*, 29 Oct. 2020, https://www.ibelieve.com/relationships/truly-harmful-effects-of-gossip.html.

CHAPTER TEN

Constructed Fate of Indian Women in Difficult Daughters

M. M. Urchavi,
I M.A. English Literature,
Sri Krishna Arts and Science College, Coimbatore

Abstract

The paper critically analyzes the concept of "constructed fate" in Manju Kapur's novel, *Difficult Daughters*, underscoring how Indian women's destinies are shaped by societal, cultural, and patriarchal hegemony. Set in pre- and post-Partition India, the novel portrays how dogmatic social expectations are, particularly in the domains of marriage, education, and familial honor, constrain women's choices and restricts their autonomy. Through the protagonist Virmati's journey, the novel highlights the tension between personal desires and socially prescribed roles, showcasing how women's agency is deliberately threatened. Despite Virmati's pursuit of education and intellectual fulfillment, her fate abides dictated by patriarchal ideologies that view marriage as a woman's ultimate destiny. Even as she resists, her struggle elucidates that confrontation alone is often deficient to tear down firmly entrenched systems. Additionally, the role of women depictions such as Kasturi, Virmati's mother, emphasizes how women themselves become enactors of subjugating ideologies, perpetuating the prevailing structures that confine them. By analyzing Virmati's experiences and the broader societal forces at play, the study scrutinizes that the fate of Indian women in *Difficult Daughters* is not a result of individual choices rather a socially constructed phenomenon that fortifies existing Gendered power dynamics. The novel, therefore, serves as both a critique of and a reflection on the limited autonomy afforded to women in traditional Indian society.

Keywords: Constructed fate, Indian women, patriarchy, education, marriage, familial honor.

Constructed Fate of Indian Women in Difficult Daughters

Introduction

The concept of "constructed fate" pertains to the societal and cultural dynamics that preordain an individual's life trajectory. In *Difficult Daughters*, Manju Kapur presents a poignant chronicle of how women's lives are conditioned by deep-rooted hegemonic masculinity. Through the character of Virmati, the novel explores the psychological strain between personal aspiration and societal expectation, illuminating how societal paradigms leave women with narrowed possibilities. Despite her determination to chase intellectual fulfillment, she remains trapped within the patriarchal structure she struggles to break free from, ultimately reinforcing the notion that resistance alone is insufficient to dismantle entrenched systems. The adversity for education, autonomy, and identity, set against the milieu of pre- and post-Partition India, becomes emblematic of the widespread repression faced by Indian women (Chatterjee 127). The paper aims to examine how fate is constructed for women in *Difficult Daughters*, demonstrating how social, cultural, and patriarchal structures dictate their lives. It also explores how women are both victims and enforcers of these societal constraints.

The Role of Patriarchy In Constructing Women's Fate

Patriarchy is a dominant force in *Difficult Daughters*, constructing not only women's roles but also their aspirations, autonomy, and life choices. The societal infrastructure presented in the novel compels Stringent stipulation on women, overpowering them to mandate marriage and maternity over self-actualization, education, and independence. From an tender age, women are conditioned to adopt that their ultimate calling is to serve as dutiful daughters, wives, and mothers, rather than aspiring their own ambitions. The protagonist, Virmati, becomes a poignant representation of this struggle as she toils to break free from the societal mold. She harbors a deep thirst for education and Intellectual gratification, yet her aspirations are incessantly confronted by the deeply entrenched male supremacy surrounding her. While she attempts to forge her own path by seeking erudition and making choices beyond prevailing norms, she is constantly reiterated that her primary duty is to marry a man and uphold familial honor, reinforcing the idea that a woman's worth is measured by her adherence to societal expectations.

The novel also underscores the role of men as enforcers of institutionalized patriarchy, explicitly or implicitly maintaining systems of control over women's lives. Virmati's father, for instance, holds the belief that education should not intrude with a woman's conjual prospects, viewing academic pursuits as secondary to the obligation of becoming a wife and mother. His stance reveals the established social paradigm that a woman's primary role is within the familial relam, where docility and atonement are more estimable than intellect and independence. Similarly, Harish, the professor with whom Virmati falls in love, at the onset he appears to hail her intellect and visions. Albeit, as their relationship progresses, it becomes overt that he, too, is bound by patriarchal ideologies. While he admires Virmati's cognitive empowerment and independent spirit, he does not seem to elevate her as an equal partner on the contrary enclosures her to the role of a second wife. His actions reflect the contradiction within androcentric systems, where men may superficially encourage women's empowerment but ultimately expect them to conform to inherited gender constructs.

Through these characters and their interactions, *Difficult Daughters* underscores the ubiquitous nature of patriarchal oppression, exemplifying how it is reinforced not just through cultural doctrines and conventions but also through hereditary and personal affiliations. Despite women like Virmati strive to defy these limitations, their struggles reveal that mere resistance is not always enough to deconstruct such deeply ingrained paradigms. Instead, the novel suggests that patriarchal ideologies persist across generations, upheld by both men and women who internalize and perpetuate these beliefs, making the fight for emancipation a convoluted and ongoing battle.

Marriage as a Tool of Social Control

In *Difficult Daughters*, marriage is depicted as both a personal and societal institution that acts as an apparatus for reinforcing social expectations, amplifying women's subjugation and limiting their freedom. Women are conditioned to see marriage as their ultimate destiny, making their value contingent on conforming to patriarchal expectations (Mohanty 75). For Virmati, marriage is not a choice but an inevitability imposed by societal norms. Despite her pursuit of education and intellectual independence, her worth is still measured by her marital status. Her attempts to forge a life beyond canonical expectations are met with resistance, as persisting in unmarried status carries a social stigma that could dishonor her family. The novel underscores how, regardless of a woman's ambition, marriage remains the defining marker of societal endorsement.

Another example of marriage as a tool of control is seen through Ganga, Harish's first wife. Given no choice in her marriage, she is expected to adhere to her designated role as a dutiful wife despite her husband's infidelity. Her passive compliance of Harish's polygamous relationship with Virmati highlights how women are accustomed to endure suffering to maintain societal order (Chatterjee 133). Ganga's situation reflects how women are expected to silence their impulses and passions for the sake of preserving familial esteem, with little recourse against marital oppression.

Through these characters, *Difficult Daughters* critiques marriage as a means of perpetuating patriarchal authority. The novel highlights how women, despite their difficulties, remain enclosed within structures designed to regulate them. Marriage, therefore, is not just a personal commitment but a societal construct that dictates women's roles, restricts their independence, and confirms the continuation of patriarchal dominance across generations.

Education vs. Societal Expectations

In *Difficult Daughters*, education emerges as one of the meager opportunities through which women attempt to challenge societal constraints, yet it remains insufficient in granting them true freedom. Virmati's pursuit of intellectual enrichment is a radical act in a sociopolitical structure that discourages female intellectualism, viewing educated women as a threat to rigid gender constructs. Her decision to pursue knowledge is met with contention from her family, who believe that a woman's primary duty is to marry and preserve familial honor. Despite these obstacles, education becomes a source of empowerment for Virmati, enabling her to build a sense of self-worth and redefine her life beyond traditional domestic confines. However, her struggle reveals that education alone does not inherently grant autonomy, as deeply entrenched patriarchal norms persist in dictating her fate.

Instead of liberating her, Virmati's education emerges as yet another battleground where she is forced to reconcile the tension between personal aspirations and societal expectations. Her relationship with Harish serves as a testament to the shortcomings of education in dismantling patriarchal structures. While Harish is an intellectual who initially appreciates Virmati's intelligence, he expects her to conform to the expectations of a wife rather than an equal partner, Despite any appearance of progressiveness, he ultimately sustains the very patriarchal norms he seems to challenge. Regardless of her academic achievements, Virmati finds herself in a subservient position within her marriage, as the institutions of marriage and family continue to define their worth. Her experiences demonstrate that while education provides women with knowledge and confidence, true empowerment calls for a profound restructuring of society that challenges the rigid structures that confine women.

Women as Enforcers of Patriarchy

One of the most striking aspects of *Difficult Daughters* is its portrayal of how women, despite being victims of patriarchy, actively perpetuate their own enslavement. The pressure to marry is not merely an expectation imposed by men but is often reinforced by women who have internalized patriarchal hierarchies. Kasturi, Virmati's mother, embodies this generational reinforcement of tradition, believing that a woman's rightful place is in her husband's home, tending to her family (Kandiyoti 278). She continuously discourages Virmati from prioritizing her education over marriage, reasserting that a daughter who is "difficult" or rebellious brings disgrace to her family. This internalized patriarchy is particularly evident in how women themselves become the enforcers and perpetuate the very ideologies that contribute to their oppression. By prioritizing marriage over education while systematically suppressing defiance, Kasturi ensures that patriarchal structures stay intact, making it difficult for women to break free from societal constraints.

This pattern is not unique to *Difficult Daughters* but is a pervasive discourse in feminist literature, where women engrained by traditional gender roles often become the strongest enforcers of them. Despite having endured the weight of these expectations herself, Kasturi propagates them, fearing that her daughter's rebellion will bring disgrace to the family's reputation among the society. Her role in molding Virmati's fate illustrates how oppression is not solely imposed by men but is sustained within families, passed down through generations. By portraying how patriarchal ideologies are reinforced by women, the novel sheds light on the deeply ingrained dynamics of gender-based repression, making the fight for autonomy even more complex and strenuous.

The Illusion of Agency

While Virmati rebels against societal precepts, her resistance is ultimately constrained by the same existing structures she seeks to escape.

Her pursuit of education and personal choice in love challenge traditional demands and expectations, yet she remains bound by the deeply ingrained patriarchal power systems that dictate women's roles. Her fate is not entirely her own; rather, it is constructed by external pressures from her family, community, and even the man she loves. Even in moments where she exercises defiance such as choosing to study rather than marry or engaging in a relationship with Harish, her actions are still controlled by a system that limits her options and ensures that any deviation from the collective doctrine comes at great personal cost.

This lack of true agency is a central theme in the novel, reflecting the overarching difficulties of women in patriarchal societies. Virmati's story illustrates how subjugation is not merely a matter of individual willpower but is embedded in societal structures that resist change. Despite her efforts to carve out a different path, she ultimately conforms to a role that still places her in a subordinate position, shedding light on how the deeply institutionalized constraints of gender expectations are. The novel does not provide a clear resolution to her struggles, reinforcing the idea that breaking free from a constructed fate is not a singular act of rebellion but a collective challenge requiring widespread societal transformation. Through Virmati's experiences, *Difficult Daughters* critiques the illusion of individual resistance, suggesting that true resolution can only be acquired when social systems evolve to support women's autonomy and independence.

Conclusion

Manju Kapur's *Difficult Daughters* manifests a compelling critique of how women's fates are socially constructed through patriarchal, cultural, and familial expectations. Through Virmati's journey, the novel highlights the limited autonomy afforded to women, demonstrating how marriage, education, and family honor serve as instruments of domination. Even as Virmati resists these restraints, her adversity ultimately underscores the ingrained rigidity of these social hierarchies, where individual defiance is often insufficient to drive about meaningful change. The novel challenges readers to reflect on how gender roles are reinforced across generations, illustrating that the systematic subjugation of women is not merely enforced by men but is also upheld by women who internalize and perpetuate patriarchal norms and ideologies. Regardless of their attempts to claim autonomy, women like Virmati remain confined within the boundaries of tradition, showing how firmly entrenched these expectations are in roots of Indian society. By portraying the complexities of female agency and oppression, *Difficult Daughters* serves as both a critique of traditional Indian social structures and a call for greater gender equality. It urges readers to question the systemic nature of gender-based restrictions and accentuates the necessity for collective social change, rather than individual resistance alone, to dismantle the cycles of deep-seated inequities that shape women's trajectories.

References

Kapur, Manju. *Difficult Daughters.* Faber & Faber, 1998.

Chatterjee, Partha. *The Nation and Its Fragments: Colonial and Postcolonial Histories.* Princeton University Press, 1993.

Kandiyoti, Deniz. "Bargaining with Patriarchy." *Gender and Society*, vol. 2, no. 3, 1988, pp. 274–290.

Mohanty, Chandra Talpade. "Under Western Eyes: Feminist Scholarship and Colonial Discourses." *Feminist Review*, vol. 30, 1988, pp. 61–88.

Dystopian Oppression and Female Resilience in Manjula Padmanabhan's Escape

Mrs. P. Devi Priya[1],
Ph.D. Research Scholar, Department of English,
Arignar Anna Govt. Arts College, Villupuram.
Dr. B. Raja Rajeswari Jayarani[2],
Research Supervisor & Guide,
Associate Professor, Department of English,
Arignar Anna Govt. Arts College, Villupuram.

Abstract

Manjula Padmanabhan is an Indian playwright, author, illustrator, and journalist known for her bold and thought-provoking works. She was born in 1953 and has made significant contributions to Indian literature, particularly in the fields of dystopian fiction and feminist themes. Manjula Padmanabhan's novel Escape (2008) presents a chilling dystopian vision of a world where women have been exterminated, leaving behind a male-dominated, authoritarian society. The novel follows Meiji, the last known female, as she struggles to survive in a world that perceives her as both a threat and a rarity. Meiji is the only girl in a dystopian world where women have been nearly wiped out. She has been raised in isolation and protected from the outside world. She struggles with questions of identity, freedom, and survival. Throughout the novel, Meiji seeks autonomy and self-discovery in a world that seeks to erase her existence. The other character is Uncle Youngest. Uncle is both a father figure and a symbol of control in Meiji's life. Uncle is Meiji's sole guardian, responsible for her survival. He is protective but also authoritative, controlling her access to the truth. He hides Meiji's identity and ensures her safety in a male-dominated society. He is a complex character, torn between protecting her and restricting her freedom. Through the lens of feminist dystopian fiction, Escape explores themes of gender oppression, surveillance, and individual resistance against a totalitarian system. This article critically examines how Padmanabhan constructs a future society that reflects contemporary concerns about gender violence, power imbalances, and the erasure of female agency.

Key words: hyper-masculine, gender, identity, oppressive society, self-determination, dominance, surveillance

Dystopian Oppression and Female Resilience in Manjula Padmanabhan's Escape

Dystopian fiction has long served as a powerful medium for critiquing social injustices and projecting contemporary anxieties into the future. Dystopian refers to an imagined or real society characterized by suffering, oppression, or injustice, often under a totalitarian government or extreme societal control. Dystopian settings typically depict bleak, dehumanizing environments where people face restricted freedoms, surveillance, or extreme inequalities. his oppression is often enforced by authoritarian governments, rigid societal structures, or advanced technological systems, leaving little to no personal freedom. Resilience refers to the ability to recover from difficulties, adapt to challenges, and persist despite adversity. It is the strength to endure hardships and overcome obstacles, whether physical, emotional, or psychological. In Escape, Manjula Padmanabhan creates a speculative world in which women have been systematically eliminated due to an unexplained purge. Dystopian oppression is evident in the way women are marginalized, controlled, and stripped of their identity, particularly in *Escape* and *The Island of Lost Girls*, where patriarchal and authoritarian forces dictate their lives.

Escape by Manjula Padmanabhan is a dystopian novel that presents a grim world where women have been nearly exterminated, leading to a society dominated entirely by men. The story revolves around Meiji, the last known surviving female, who is secretly raised and protected by three Uncles. They shield her from the outside world, fearing the brutal fate she would face if discovered. However, Meiji, curious and restless, begins to question her confinement and yearns for freedom. As she grows older, the Uncles realize that keeping her hidden is no longer a safe option, and they decide to help her escape to an unknown land where she might find safety. The novel follows her perilous journey through a harsh, patriarchal world where she encounters danger, betrayal, and the constant threat of capture. Meiji's struggle represents the resilience and resistance of women against oppressive systems. Through Meiji's story, *Escape* explores themes of gender discrimination, survival, and the fight for self-identity. The novel critiques extreme patriarchy, showing how oppression leads to a loss of humanity and individuality. Meiji's journey symbolizes hope, as she refuses to be erased and fights to claim her existence despite overwhelming odds.

The most striking aspect of *Escape* is its dystopian premise: a world entirely devoid of women, except for one—Meiji. The novel portrays a hyper-masculine, authoritarian regime that monitors and suppresses any deviation from its rigid control. The extermination of women is not merely a plot device but a commentary on the real-world threats to female autonomy and the persistent struggles against patriarchal dominance. Meiji's existence is concealed by her three uncles—Elder, Middle, and Youngest—who recognize both the danger and necessity of her survival. Her presence challenges the foundations of a society that has normalized the absence of women.

In *Escape* by Manjula Padmanabhan, Meiji embodies female resilience in a dystopian world dominated by patriarchal oppression. Her character represents resistance, survival, and the struggle for self-determination in a society where women have been nearly exterminated. Here are key aspects of Meiji's resilience:

Survival in a Hostile World

Meiji grows up in isolation, protected by the three Uncles who shield her from the oppressive system. Despite this, she develops a strong will to survive and an innate curiosity about the outside world. Her ability to navigate dangers reflects her resilience.

Challenging the Status Quo

Unlike the Uncles, who want to keep her hidden for her safety, Meiji longs for freedom and knowledge. Her desire to explore and escape from confinement is an act of defiance against the oppressive world that seeks to erase women.

Endurance in Adversity

As Meiji embarks on her journey beyond the safe zone, she faces numerous hardships, including physical threats and psychological trauma. Her ability to endure these challenges without surrendering to despair showcases her resilience.

Symbol of Hope and Resistance

Meiji represents the possibility of change in a world that has dehumanized women. Her survival and defiance make her a symbol of female strength, echoing the struggles of women throughout history who have fought against patriarchal oppression.

Overall, Meiji's resilience in Escape is a testament to the indomitable spirit of women who resist control, seek freedom, and assert their identity despite overwhelming odds. The novel emphasizes the omnipresence of state surveillance, where every movement is monitored, and nonconformity is met with severe consequences. This aspect of Escape draws parallels to contemporary concerns about mass surveillance, loss of privacy, and authoritarian control. The oppressive regime enforces conformity through strict laws, manipulating information to sustain its power.

Meiji's Journey: Rebellion and the Quest for Freedom

The central narrative of Escape revolves around Meiji's journey from captivity to self-awareness. Her uncles, particularly Youngest, arrange for her escape, setting her on a perilous path that forces her to confront the dangers of the outside world. Her journey symbolizes resistance against systemic oppression and the fight for self-determination.

Padmanabhan crafts Meiji as a reluctant yet determined protagonist, representing the resilience of marginalized voices. Her character development highlights the transition from passivity to agency, a key theme in feminist dystopian literature.

Feminist Dystopia and Real-World Parallels

Padmanabhan's novel aligns with the feminist dystopian tradition seen in works like Margaret Atwood's The Handmaid's Tale. Both novels critique gender-based oppression, emphasizing the fragility of women's rights in the face of authoritarian control.

Moreover, Escape resonates with real-world issues such as gender violence, selective gender erasure (as seen in cases of female infanticide), and the societal control of women's bodies. By envisioning a future devoid of women, the novel serves as a cautionary tale about the consequences of unchecked misogyny.

Conclusion

Manjula Padmanabhan's *Escape* is a haunting exploration of a dystopian world that exaggerates contemporary gender anxieties to provoke thought and debate. Through Meiji's journey, the novel interrogates themes of oppression, survival, and resistance, making it a crucial addition to feminist dystopian literature. Padmanabhan's sharp critique of patriarchal power structures forces readers to reflect on the fragility of gender rights and the ongoing struggles for equality. By examining Escape in the context of dystopian fiction, this article underscores its relevance as a work that not only entertains but also challenges societal norms and injustices. The novel's powerful message serves as a reminder that the erasure of any group—whether by systemic violence or ideological control—poses a threat to the fabric of humanity itself.

Works Cited:

Ara, A. (2022). Gender Studies in Works of Manjula Padmanabhan, The Criterion: An International Journal in English, 13 (I), 167–175. (In English)

Basu, A., & Tripathi, P. (2023). Beyond Reproduction: An Epistemological Search for a "Woman" in Manjula Padmanabhan's Escape and The Island of Lost Girls. *Acta Universitatis Sapientiae, Philologica, 15,* 37–53. https://doi.org/10.2478/ausp-2023-0003

Padmanabhan, Manjula. Escape. Picador India, 2008.

Pandey, Shramita. "Uma Parameswaran and Manjula Padmanabhan: A Study in Theme and Characterization" http://shodhganga.inflibnet.ac.in/handle/10603/70319

Eco critical Readings of Nature in "Mother of Pearl" by Melinda Haynes :Examining the Intersection of Environmental Justice and Peripheral Geographies

R.Deepa[1],
Assistant Professor of English,
Sir Issac Newton College of Engineering and Technology,
Nagapattinam, Tamilnadu.
S.Suseeladevi[2],
Assistant Professor of English,
Sir Issac Newton College of Engineering and Technology,
Nagapattinam, Tamilnadu.

Abstract:

Melinda Haynes' Mother of Pearl delves deeply into the complex themes of race, identity, and the nuanced relationships between marginalized communities and their environments in the American South. Through an Eco-critical lens, the novel weaves together the personal struggles of its characters with the broader social and environmental degradation they endure. Set in the rural South, Haynes reveals the ecological consequences of historical oppression, colonial legacies, and socio-economic inequalities.

The land, often depicted as barren and exploited, becomes a poignant symbol of the emotional and cultural scars left by centuries of racial injustice and segregation. In this narrative, the characters' journeys for survival and self-discovery mirror the extensive environmental destruction caused by industrialization and systemic racism. The tension between the natural world and the forces of capitalism, colonialism, and exploitation is palpable, as the land stands as both a site of resistance and a testament to cultural heritage. Haynes skillfully contrasts her characters' personal traumas with the ecological crises surrounding them, highlighting the intricate connections between colonization and the struggles faced by marginalized areas. The novel serves as a critical examination of environmental justice, showcasing how the rural South's disenfranchised communities fight for both social equity and the preservation of their vital landscapes. It prompts readers to reflect on how colonial and postcolonial histories shape not only human experiences but also the environment, urging a contemplation of the intersections of race, history, and ecology in postcolonial literature. Through Mother of Pearl, Haynes presents a powerful narrative that emphasizes the urgent need to reclaim cultural autonomy alongside environmental stewardship.

Keywords: Eco criticism , Environmental Justice ,Colonial Legacies ,Peripheral Geographies , Rural South ,Environmental Degradation

Eco critical Readings of Nature in "Mother of Pearl" by Melinda Haynes :Examining the Intersection of Environmental Justice and Peripheral Geographies

Introduction

Postcolonial eco-criticism investigates the ways in which literature addresses the intersection of environmental degradation and historical injustices rooted in colonial and racial hierarchies. In *Mother of Pearl*, Haynes crafts a setting where nature serves as both sanctuary and site of oppression, reflecting broader environmental injustices faced by marginalized communities. This paper examines how Haynes' depiction of nature aligns with contemporary debates in environmental justice, particularly as they relate to peripheral geographies shaped by racial and socio-economic disparities. This paper looks at how nature is portrayed in a book called "Mother of Pearl" by Melinda Haynes. It explores how the environment in the story reflects real-world issues of unfairness and mistreatment, especially for communities that have been historically disadvantaged. The analysis considers how the book's depiction of nature relates to current discussions about environmental justice, particularly in areas affected by racial and economic inequalities.

Theoretical Framework

The analysis of *Mother of Pearl* is informed by two primary critical lenses: postcolonial ecocriticism and environmental justice theory. Drawing from theorists such as Rob Nixon and Elizabeth DeLoughrey, this study considers how slow violence, ecological marginalization, and colonial histories shape the environmental consciousness of the novel's characters.

Nature as Refuge and Resistance

One of the central eco-critical themes in *Mother of Pearl* is the dual role of nature as both a site of refuge and resistance. Nature, particularly the Southern wilderness, becomes a liminal space where characters like Even Grade, a Black orphan, and Valuable Korner, a white teenager, seek solace and self-definition. However, this natural world is not immune to the racial and economic hierarchies that govern human society. Instead, it reflects the structural inequalities that define the postcolonial South.

Environmental Justice and Peripheral Geographies

Peripheral geographies in postcolonial literature often highlight the uneven distribution of environmental benefits and burdens. In *Mother of Pearl*, racialized spaces—such as the swamps and isolated landscapes—are depicted as both liberating and confining. The novel underscores how systemic racism and economic disenfranchisement render Black and poor white communities particularly vulnerable to environmental precarity.

Colonial Legacies and Ecological Degradation

A crucial aspect of postcolonial ecocriticism is its focus on the lingering effects of colonial exploitation on land and people. Haynes' Mississippi landscape bears the scars of historical extractivism, with depleted resources mirroring the socio-political exhaustion of its inhabitants. The novel implicitly critiques the plantation legacy that has left environmental and social destruction in its wake, situating its characters within a continuum of dispossession and ecological dislocation. The novel's exploration of environmental injustice extends beyond the immediate effects of systemic racism and economic disenfranchisement, delving into the intergenerational trauma inflicted upon marginalized communities. Haynes' portrayal of the Mississippi landscape as a site of both liberation and confinement speaks to the complex relationship between people and place, where the environment simultaneously offers refuge from oppression and serves as a stark reminder of historical and ongoing inequalities.

The postcolonial ecocritical lens employed in Mother of Pearl invites readers to consider how the legacy of colonialism continues to shape both the physical landscape and the social dynamics of the region. By intertwining the narratives of ecological degradation and human exploitation, Haynes illuminates the interconnectedness of environmental and social justice issues, challenging readers to confront the lasting impacts of historical injustices on present-day communities and ecosystems.

Conclusion

By engaging with *Mother of Pearl* through an eco-critical and postcolonial framework, this paper reveals the novel's contribution to environmental justice discourse. Haynes' depiction of nature, embedded within racial and socio-economic struggles, offers a nuanced exploration of how peripheral geographies function as both sites of oppression and survival. This study ultimately underscores the importance of integrating environmental justice within postcolonial literary studies, recognizing the ecological dimensions of historical and contemporary injustices. Haynes' Mississippi landscape serves as a powerful metaphorical representation of the complex intersection between environmental exploitation and social inequity. The author skillfully portrays a terrain that has been profoundly shaped by centuries of resource extraction and systemic oppression, creating a vivid backdrop against which the characters must navigate their lives. This carefully crafted setting not only provides a physical context for the narrative but also serves as a reflection of the deeper societal issues at play.

References

Haynes, Melinda. *Mother of Pearl*. Hyperion, 1999.Primary text for analysis.

Nixon, Rob. *Slow Violence and the Environmentalism of the Poor*. Harvard University Press, 2011.Discusses the concept of slow violence and how marginalized communities suffer from environmental injustices over time.

DeLoughrey, Elizabeth, and George B. Handley (Eds.). *Postcolonial Ecologies: Literatures of the Environment*. Oxford University Press, 2011.

Huggan, Graham, and Helen Tiffin. *Postcolonial Ecocriticism: Literature, Animals, Environment*. Routledge, 2010.Provides foundational theories for postcolonial ecocriticism.

Adamson, Joni, Mei Mei Evans, and Rachel Stein (Eds.). *The Environmental Justice Reader: Politics, Poetics, and Pedagogy*. University of Arizona Press, 2002.

CHAPTER THIRTEEN

Indigenous Knowledge in Decolonial Movements Reclaiming Cultural Sovereignty in Salman Rushdie's Midnight's Children

S.Suseela Devi[1],
Assistant Professor of English,
Sir Issac Newton College of Engineering and Technology,
Nagapattinam, Tamilnadu.
R.Deepa[2],
Assistant Professor of English,
Sir Issac Newton College of Engineering and Technology,
Nagapattinam, Tamilnadu.

Abstract

Salman Rushdie's "Midnight's Children" offers a profound examination of postcolonial identity, cultural autonomy, and the intricacies of decolonial efforts amid globalization. Set during the pivotal moments of India's independence and partition, the story centres on Saleem Sinai, whose birth coincides with the nation's newfound freedom, intertwining his life with the trajectory of India itself? Utilizing magical realism, Rushdie explores the complex interplay between indigenous knowledge, colonial histories, and the on-going quest for self-determination. The narrative intricately blends historical events, folklore, and myth, showcasing India's rich cultural diversity and the enduring strength of indigenous traditions in the face of Western colonialism and its lingering impacts in a globalized context.In "Midnight's Children," Rushdie critiques the encroachment of Western modernity and its efforts to diminish or overlook indigenous knowledge systems. The novel illustrates how the colonization of the Indian subcontinent disrupted the cultural and spiritual continuity of its inhabitants, while simultaneously highlighting the resilience of these traditions in the postcolonial landscape. By connecting personal experiences with broader political themes, Rushdie reveals the friction between traditional and contemporary knowledge systems, as well as the difficulties in reclaiming cultural sovereignty in a globalized world. Through the journeys of Saleem and his fellow "Midnight's Children," the narrative emphasizes the significance of honouring indigenous cultural legacies as essential to decolonial movements, ultimately portraying a story of resistance where reclaiming identity, history, and knowledge is crucial for confronting the on-going ramifications of colonialism.

Keywords: Reclaiming History, Hybridity, Spiritual Continuity, Narrative as Resistance, Resistance and Reclamation, Diaspora, Indian Independence, Historical Fiction

Indigenous Knowledge in Decolonial Movements Reclaiming Cultural Sovereignty in Salman Rushdie's Midnight's Children

Introduction

Decolonial movements across the globe have increasingly turned to Indigenous Knowledge Systems (IKS) to reclaim autonomy over cultural identity, governance, and epistemology. Globalization, while offering connectivity and economic opportunities, also threatens indigenous cultures through assimilation and erasure. Literature serves as a powerful tool in this struggle, offering a space to critique colonial legacies and assert indigenous worldviews. Salman Rushdie's *Midnight's Children* exemplifies this role by interweaving history, mythology, and personal narrative to challenge colonial and postcolonial paradigms. This paper examines how Rushdie's novel informs contemporary decolonial discourse and the ways in which IKS provide frameworks for resisting cultural displacement. By blending magical realism with historical events, Rushdie creates a narrative landscape that resists linear, Western-centric interpretations of India's past and present. The novel's protagonist, Saleem Sinai, embodies the complexities of postcolonial identity, his telepathic abilities serving as a metaphor for the interconnectedness of individual and collective experiences. Through Saleem's journey, Rushdie explores the tension between national unity and cultural diversity, challenging the notion of a singular, homogeneous Indian identity in the wake of colonial rule.

Indigenous Knowledge Systems as Tools for Decolonization

IKS encompass traditional ecological knowledge, oral histories, spirituality, and governance structures that have sustained communities for centuries. These systems are not static but dynamic, evolving to meet contemporary challenges. Decolonization efforts, from language revitalization projects to land reclamation movements, often hinge on the reassertion of these knowledge systems. By exploring indigenous narratives, we can understand the epistemological resistance embedded within them and their role in fostering cultural resilience. Indigenous Knowledge Systems (IKS) offer a powerful counternarrative to colonial epistemologies, providing alternative frameworks for understanding the world and human relationships with nature. These systems challenge the hegemony of Western scientific thought by presenting holistic approaches that integrate spiritual, ecological, and social dimensions of knowledge.

The incorporation of IKS into decolonization efforts represents a reclamation of cultural identity and sovereignty. By centring indigenous ways of knowing in education, policy-making, and environmental management, communities can resist the ongoing impacts of colonialism and forge pathways towards self-determination and sustainable development.

Midnight's Children and the Politics of Memory

Rushdie's *Midnight's Children* serves as an allegory for India's postcolonial identity crisis, intertwining personal memory with national history. The protagonist, Saleem Sinai, embodies the fragmentation of identity caused by colonialism and the struggle to reconstruct meaning in its aftermath. This novel illustrates how storytelling acts as an indigenous epistemological tool, preserving cultural knowledge and challenging colonial historiographies. Rushdie's use of magical realism reflects indigenous storytelling traditions, which often integrate the supernatural with historical reality, reinforcing the legitimacy of non-Western worldviews. Through his innovative narrative technique, Rushdie masterfully intertwines personal and collective memories, crafting an intricate tapestry that vividly reflects the multifaceted nature of postcolonial identity. This skilful interplay between individual experiences and broader national histories serves to underscore the critical importance of indigenous storytelling in preserving cultural heritage and actively resisting dominant colonial narratives. By wholeheartedly embracing the genre of magical realism, Rushdie not only challenges established Western literary conventions but also validates and elevates indigenous ways of knowing and understanding the world.

The author's approach to storytelling goes beyond mere recounting of events, instead creating a rich, layered narrative that mirrors the complexity of postcolonial societies. By blending personal anecdotes with historical events, Rushdie creates a narrative space where individual voices contribute to a larger, collective story. This technique allows readers to engage with the text on multiple levels, simultaneously experiencing intimate personal journeys and sweeping national sagas.

Rushdie's use of magical realism serves as a powerful tool for exploring the nuances of postcolonial identity. By blurring the lines between reality and fantasy, he creates a narrative landscape where the extraordinary becomes ordinary, reflecting the often surreal experiences of those navigating the aftermath of colonialism. This approach not only challenges Western literary norms but also provides a means of expressing cultural experiences that may not fit neatly into conventional narrative structures.

Furthermore, Rushdie's work emphasizes the crucial role of indigenous storytelling in maintaining cultural continuity and resisting the erasure often associated with colonial narratives. By incorporating elements of oral tradition, folklore, and local myths into his writing, he validates these forms of knowledge and preserves them for future generations. This act of literary preservation becomes a form of cultural resistance, asserting the value and validity of indigenous perspectives in the face of dominant Western narratives.

In essence, Rushdie's narrative technique serves as a powerful vehicle for exploring and expressing the complexities of postcolonial identity. By weaving together personal and collective experiences, embracing magical realism, and championing indigenous storytelling, he creates a literary space that challenges, preserves, and celebrates the diverse voices and experiences of postcolonial societies.

Reclaiming Cultural Sovereignty in the Face of Globalization

Globalization often imposes Western-centric narratives that marginalize indigenous perspectives. However, decolonial movements have leveraged both traditional knowledge and modern technology to resist cultural erosion. Digital platforms have become spaces for indigenous activism, promoting language preservation, indigenous governance models, and epistemic justice. Literature, including *Midnight's Children*, functions within this broader discourse, demonstrating the potential for storytelling to act as a form of cultural sovereignty. Rushdie's masterful blending of magical elements with historical events not only pays homage to indigenous storytelling traditions but also challenges the dominance of Western literary conventions. This narrative technique serves as a powerful tool for reclaiming cultural identity and asserting the validity of alternative worldviews in the face of globalization's homogenizing forces.

The intersection of traditional knowledge and modern technology in decolonial movements exemplifies the dynamic nature of cultural resistance. By utilizing digital platforms for language preservation and promoting indigenous governance models, these movements demonstrate the adaptability and resilience of indigenous cultures in the contemporary world. In this context, works like Midnight's Children contribute to a broader cultural dialogue, illustrating how literature can serve as a potent medium for asserting cultural sovereignty and challenging established power structures.

Conclusion

Indigenous Knowledge Systems offer invaluable insights for decolonial movements, enabling communities to reclaim autonomy in the face of globalization's homogenizing pressures. Salman Rushdie's *Midnight's Children* provides a literary framework to examine these struggles, highlighting the importance of memory, language, and storytelling in cultural resistance. By integrating IKS into decolonial strategies, societies can move toward more inclusive and diverse epistemologies, ensuring that indigenous voices remain central in shaping the future.

References

Rushdie, S. (1981). Midnight's Children. Jonathan Cape.

Kabir, A. J. (2023). Grooving on at Seventy-Five: Shah Rukh Khan, Salman Rushdie, and the Indian Muslim's ecstatic return. South Asian Review, 45(1–2), 6–21. https://doi.org/10.1080/02759527.2023.2262789

Smale, D. (2002). Salman Rushdie: Midnight's Children - The Satanic Verses. http://ci.nii.ac.jp/ncid/BA71033626

CHAPTER FOURTEEN

Silent Sufferers: Themes of Marginalization in Anita Desai's Fiction

N.Subramaniyan[1],
Assistant Professor of English,
Arifa Institute of Technology,
Esanoor, Nagapattinam, Tamilnadu
Jeeva Micheal Raj.L[2],
Assistant Professor of English,
Arifa Institute of Technology,
Esanoor, Nagapattinam, Tamilnadu

Abstract

Anita Desai's fiction poignantly explores themes of marginalization, focusing on the silent suffering of individuals who are pushed to the periphery of society. Her narratives vividly portray the struggles of women, the elderly, and those caught between tradition and modernity, shedding light on their psychological isolation and societal alienation. Through characters like Maya in *Cry, the Peacock*, Bim in *Clear Light of Day*, and Nanda Kaul in *Fire on the Mountain*, Desai highlights the emotional turmoil faced by women resisting patriarchal norms and the elderly abandoned by their families. Additionally, her works such as *Baumgartner's Bombay* and *In Custody* reflect the displacement experienced by individuals grappling with cultural transitions and the decline of traditional identities.

Beyond external marginalization, Desai delves into the psychological dimensions of isolation, illustrating how internal conflicts contribute to human suffering. Her introspective storytelling reveals the complexities of alienation, emphasizing that marginalization is not just a social condition but also a deeply personal experience. This article examines how Desai's literary exploration of silent sufferers serves as a critique of societal norms while offering profound psychological insights. Her work remains relevant in contemporary discussions on gender, age, culture, and identity, making her a crucial literary figure in the discourse on social alienation.

Keywords: Marginalization, Isolation, Alienation, Patriarchy, Psychological Conflict, Gender Oppression, Cultural Displacement, Tradition vs. Modernity, Silent Suffering, Anita Desai, Indian English Literature, Identity Crisis, Social Alienation, Existential Struggle.

Silent Sufferers: Themes of Marginalization in Anita Desai's Fiction
Introduction

Anita Desai, one of the most profound and insightful voices in Indian English literature, has carved a niche for herself with her evocative storytelling and deep psychological exploration of characters. Her novels often center around themes of isolation, alienation, and marginalization, shedding light on individuals who suffer silently on the fringes of society. Be it women struggling under patriarchal oppression, the elderly facing loneliness, or individuals grappling with cultural displacement, Desai's fiction exposes the emotional and psychological turmoil of those who are often unheard.

Through her delicate yet powerful prose, she reveals how external social forces, as well as internal psychological conflicts, shape human suffering. Her narratives transcend time and geography, making the issues of marginalization and silent suffering universally relatable.

Women and Marginalization

Women's oppression and marginalization are central concerns in Desai's works. Many of her female protagonists struggle against societal norms that confine them to subservient roles. In *Cry, the Peacock* (1963), Maya's psychological isolation stems from her restrictive marriage, where she is expected to conform to societal expectations rather than pursue personal fulfillment. Her descent into madness is symbolic of the silencing and erasure women often experience in patriarchal societies.

Similarly, *Clear Light of Day* (1980) presents Bim, a fiercely independent woman who resists the traditional roles expected of her. Unlike her sister Tara, who chooses marriage and social conformity, Bim remains unmarried, dedicating herself to caring for her autistic brother. Her choice, however, leads to emotional estrangement from her family, highlighting the price women often pay for asserting their independence. Desai portrays how women who refuse to adhere to societal norms are often left emotionally isolated, even within their own homes.

Another striking example is Sita from *Where Shall We Go This Summer?* (1975), who feels suffocated by the monotonous routine of domestic life. She attempts to escape her existence by fleeing to an island, symbolizing her desperate need for freedom. However, her rebellion remains internalized, and her return to conventional life underscores the inescapable constraints placed on women.

Through these narratives, Desai exposes the invisible suffering of women who either conform to or resist societal norms, highlighting the deep-rooted gender biases that persist in both traditional and modern settings.

The Aged and the Forgotten

Anita Desai frequently explores the alienation of the elderly, a theme poignantly illustrated in *Fire on the Mountain* (1977). The protagonist, Nanda Kaul, withdraws from the world after a lifetime of fulfilling familial and social obligations. She seeks solitude in the quiet hills of Kasauli, believing that she can finally escape human connections. However, her forced re-engagement with society, in the form of her great-granddaughter Raka, disrupts her self-imposed exile, making her realize that true isolation is unattainable.

This novel reflects the broader issue of elderly neglect, where aging individuals are often forgotten or cast aside by their families once they are deemed unproductive. Nanda Kaul's retreat symbolizes the internalization of this neglect, showing how the elderly sometimes impose isolation on themselves as a defense mechanism against emotional pain.

Similarly, in *Fasting, Feasting* (1999), Desai portrays old age as a time of invisibility and resignation. Uma's parents, once figures of authority, gradually fade into the background as their children pursue their own lives. Their diminished presence in the household symbolizes the loss of relevance that many elderly individuals experience in a fast-changing world.

Through these stories, Desai critiques a society that often fails to provide emotional and social support to its aging population, leaving them to suffer in silent despair.

The Burden of Tradition and Modernity

A common thread in Desai's fiction is the struggle between tradition and modernity, which often leads to a sense of displacement and marginalization. This theme is powerfully illustrated in *Baumgartner's Bombay* (1988), where Hugo Baumgartner, a Jewish refugee, fails to find a true sense of belonging in India. His alienation is twofold—both as a foreigner in a country that remains indifferent to his plight and as a man caught between cultures. His tragic fate underscores the loneliness of those who exist in liminal spaces, unable to fully integrate into any society.

Similarly, *In Custody* (1984) examines the decline of Urdu language and culture through the eyes of Deven Sharma, a small-town lecturer. His attempts to document the fading legacy of Urdu poetry end in disillusionment, highlighting the struggle of individuals whose identities are tied to vanishing traditions. His failure is emblematic of the broader cultural shift that marginalizes traditional knowledge and artistic heritage in favor of modern aspirations.

Desai's treatment of these themes reflects the painful reality of individuals who are unable to reconcile their personal identities with the evolving world around them, leaving them emotionally adrift.

Psychological Isolation and Internal Marginalization

Beyond societal factors, Desai deeply explores the internal struggles that contribute to marginalization. Many of her protagonists suffer from existential crises, feeling trapped by their circumstances and unable to escape their emotional turmoil. This theme is most evident in *Cry, the Peacock*, where Maya's descent into madness is not solely a result of external oppression but also of her internal fears and anxieties.

In *Journey to Ithaca* (1995), the spiritual quest of Matteo, an Italian man who comes to India in search of enlightenment, highlights another form of psychological alienation. His disillusionment with both Western materialism and Eastern spirituality leaves him in an existential limbo, emphasizing how internal conflicts can be just as isolating as societal rejection.

These narratives illustrate how emotional suffering often stems from within, as characters wrestle with their desires, fears, and insecurities. Desai's ability to probe the subconscious mind of her protagonists makes her fiction not only socially relevant but also deeply psychological.

Conclusion

Anita Desai masterfully captures the silent suffering of marginalized individuals, shedding light on the invisible struggles of women, the elderly, and those caught between tradition and modernity. Her narratives resonate with readers across cultures and generations, as they delve into universal themes of isolation, displacement, and the quest for identity.

By giving voice to the silenced, Desai not only critiques societal structures that perpetuate marginalization but also invites readers to engage with the inner lives of those often overlooked. Her fiction serves as both a mirror and a lens—reflecting the harsh realities of marginalization while offering a profound exploration of human emotions.

Through her deeply introspective storytelling, Desai urges us to listen to the silent sufferers among us, making her one of the most significant literary figures in the discourse on social alienation in Indian and global literature.

References:

Primary Sources (Novels by Anita Desai)

Desai, Anita. *Cry, the Peacock*. Delhi: Orient Paperbacks, 1963.

Desai, Anita. *Clear Light of Day*. London: Heinemann, 1980.

Desai, Anita. *Fire on the Mountain*. Delhi: Arnold-Heinemann, 1977.

Desai, Anita. *Where Shall We Go This Summer?* Delhi: Orient Paperbacks, 1975.

Desai, Anita. *Fasting, Feasting*. London: Chatto & Windus, 1999.

Desai, Anita. *Baumgartner's Bombay*. London: Heinemann, 1988.

Desai, Anita. *In Custody*. London: Heinemann, 1984.

Desai, Anita. *Journey to Ithaca*. London: Heinemann, 1995.

Secondary Sources (Critical Studies and Analyses)

Bande, Usha. *The Novels of Anita Desai: A Study in Character and Conflict*. New Delhi: Prestige Books, 1988.

Dhawan, R.K., ed. *The Fiction of Anita Desai*. New Delhi: Bahri Publications, 1989.

Pathak, R.S. *Modern Indian Novel in English: A Study of Anita Desai and Kamala Markandaya*. New Delhi: Creative Books, 1999.

Sharma, R.S. *Anita Desai: The Novelist and Her Novels*. Jaipur: Book Enclave, 2003.

Sree, S. Prasanna. *Alien Among Us: Reflections of Women Writers on Women*. New Delhi: Sarup & Sons, 2008.

Digital Subalternity: Social Media as a New Literary Space for the Marginalized

Dr. S. Balamurugan,
Assistant Professor of English,
Career Development Centre, Directorate of Career Centre,
SRM Institute of Science and Technology, Kattankulathur – 603 203.

Abstract

The digital age has redefined the contours of literary expression, offering marginalized communities an unprecedented platform for self-representation and resistance. This chapter explores the emergence of digital subalternity, where social media functions as an alternative literary space for the voices historically relegated to the periphery. In an era where mainstream narratives often silence or distort the lived realities of subaltern groups, digital platforms such as Twitter, Facebook, and YouTube have facilitated the articulation of counter-narratives that challenge hegemonic discourses. This chapter investigates how the subaltern reclaims authorship and reshapes the parameters of literary creation via the analysis of a few case studies and digital literary manifestations, such as hashtag activism and viral storytelling. The discussions focus on how online poetry, blogging, and digital storytelling provide new forms of cultural assertion, visibility, and resistance. The chapter also examines the constraints of digital subalternity, including problems like algorithmic prejudice, the digital divide, and the commodification of marginalized voices. Ultimately, this chapter underscores the transformative potential of social media as a literary sphere where the subaltern not only speaks but also writes, narrates, and reclaims agency in the virtual public sphere. By situating digital narratives within the broader discourse of subaltern studies and literary dimensions, this work contributes to an evolving understanding of literature beyond conventional textual boundaries, paving the way for a more inclusive and democratized literary landscape.

Key Words: *Digital Subalternity, Narrative Agency, Algorithmic Gatekeeping, Social Media Activism, Multimedia Storytelling, Platform Capitalism, Epistemic Justice*

Digital Subalternity: Social Media as a New Literary Space for the Marginalized

Introduction

Literature has historically been shaped by dominant narratives, often marginalizing voices from the periphery. The subaltern—those systematically excluded from hegemonic discourse have long struggled for representation in traditional literary canons (Spivak, 1988). However, the advent of digital technology has redefined the boundaries of literary expression, offering a dynamic and democratized space for those historically silenced. Social media platforms such as Twitter, Facebook, YouTube, and Instagram have emerged as alternative literary spheres, allowing the subaltern to articulate their narratives, challenge institutionalized hierarchies, and reclaim agency in the global discourse. This chapter explores the concept of digital subalternity, examining how social media functions as a transformative literary space for marginalized voices.

Digital storytelling has evolved as a critical mode of resistance, reshaping the ways in which literature is produced, disseminated, and consumed. The interactive nature of digital platforms fosters a participatory literary culture where personal testimonies, hashtag movements, microfiction, and visual narratives serve as instruments of socio-political change (Couldry, 2010). Movements such as #MeToo, #DalitLivesMatter, and #SayHerName have demonstrated how digital literary activism can challenge structural oppression while amplifying subaltern voices in unprecedented ways (Banaji & Bhat, 2020). These virtual spaces have enabled individuals from historically disenfranchised communities such as Dalits, Indigenous groups, LGBTQ+ individuals, and refugees to construct counter-narratives that resist erasure and exclusion.

Despite its revolutionary potential, digital subalternity is not without its challenges. Structural inequalities persist in the form of the digital divide, algorithmic bias, and corporate control over online content (Noble, 2018). The very platforms that enable subaltern expression also impose limitations through content moderation policies, data surveillance, and selective visibility. Furthermore, the commodification of subaltern narratives in digital capitalism raises critical questions about authenticity, representation, and exploitation. Thus, while social media offers a powerful medium for marginalized voices, it is essential to critically examine its affordances and constraints within the broader discourse of digital humanities and postcolonial studies.

This chapter delves into the intersections of subaltern studies, digital media, and literary theory to analyse how the virtual public sphere (Habermas, 1989) reconfigures traditional literary spaces. This chapter aims to contribute to the evolving discourse on digital subalternity through investigating case studies of digital activism, user-generated literary expressions, and the subversive potential of online storytelling. In doing so, it underscores the necessity of reimagining literary spaces in the digital age, where the subaltern not only speaks but also writes, narrates, and reclaims the power of storytelling.

2.The Subaltern Speaks Online: Reclaiming Narrative Agency

For centuries, the subaltern has remained voiceless in mainstream literary and historical discourse, with their lived experiences often mediated through elite perspectives (Spivak, 1988). The advent of digital platforms, however, has disrupted this long-standing erasure, offering the marginalized a space to articulate their narratives, contest dominant ideologies, and reclaim narrative agency. Unlike traditional literary spaces that have been largely exclusionary, social media facilitates direct and unmediated storytelling, enabling subaltern voices to emerge in ways that were previously unthinkable.

2.1. Digital Storytelling as Counter-Hegemonic Discourse

Digital platforms have become a new-age literary repository where personal testimonies, microfiction, and collective storytelling function as forms of resistance literature (Couldry, 2010). Marginalized individuals use social media to craft autoethnographic narratives, positioning themselves as active agents of history rather than passive subjects of elite historiography. For instance, Dalit activists in India have increasingly turned to Twitter and YouTube to share their experiences, mobilize resistance, and challenge casteist oppression (Rao, 2019). Similarly, Indigenous communities worldwide have embraced digital storytelling to document oral histories, preserving their cultural heritage while simultaneously asserting political autonomy (Wilson, 2018).

The interactive nature of digital platforms also fosters a participatory literary culture, where narratives are not just consumed but collectively shaped. Hashtag movements such as #DalitLivesMatter, #SayHerName, and #MeToo exemplify this shift, transforming individual experiences into collective digital archives that challenge hegemonic silence (Banaji & Bhat, 2020). These movements illustrate how digital subalternity transcends personal storytelling, evolving into a powerful form of networked activism that reconfigures the relationship between literature, politics, and social justice.

2.2. From Text to Multimedia: Expanding the Literary Spectrum

Beyond textual narratives, social media has also expanded literary expression through visual, oral, and performative storytelling. Platforms such as YouTube, Instagram, and TikTok allow subaltern voices to employ multimodal narratives, integrating spoken word poetry, digital art, and video documentation to convey their lived realities (Jenkins et al., 2013). For example, Indigenous poets and artists use TikTok to revive traditional folklore, blending oral traditions with modern digital aesthetics to reach a global audience. This shift challenges conventional notions of literature, positioning digital platforms as legitimate literary spaces that democratize storytelling beyond print culture.

Moreover, podcasting has emerged as a critical medium for subaltern literary expression, allowing marginalized communities to bypass traditional gatekeeping mechanisms in publishing and academia. Podcasts such as *All My Relations* (which explores Native American identity) and *The Caste in Culture Podcast* (which discusses caste oppression) exemplify how digital spaces facilitate nuanced and authentic subaltern discourse (Srinivasan, 2021). Unlike mainstream literary circuits that often demand linguistic conformity and formalized structures, these platforms embrace vernacular dialects and grassroots storytelling, further amplifying subaltern agency.

2.3. The Future of Digital Subalternity

Social media is transforming subaltern literary expressions, allowing marginalized voices to reclaim narrative agency and challenge dominant discourses. However, ensuring equitable participation requires engagement with digital justice, platform ethics, and preserving grassroots storytelling traditions. Recognizing digital storytelling as a legitimate literary form can contribute to a more inclusive, democratized, and transformative literary landscape.

3.Hashtags as Literature

In the contemporary digital landscape, the hashtag has emerged as a literary and rhetorical device that encapsulates collective voices, amplifies marginalized narratives, and redefines the contours of activism. Hashtags function as compressed textual artifacts, distilling complex socio-political realities into concise yet potent expressions that traverse digital spaces with unprecedented velocity. Much like poetry, hashtags rely on brevity, symbolism, and intertextuality, creating a linguistic economy that fosters engagement, solidarity, and resistance (Bruns & Burgess, 2015). This transformation of hashtags into literary instruments situates them within a new paradigm of digital subalternity, where marginalized voices, long excluded from traditional literary and historical canons, reclaim visibility and agency through networked storytelling.

3.1. The Hashtag as a Literary Form

Just as literary traditions have historically employed epigrams, aphorisms, and slogans to articulate dissent, hashtags encapsulate entire movements within a single textual unit. The syntactic structure of hashtags—marked by concatenation, capitalization, and abbreviation—evokes the stylistic features of experimental poetry and concrete literature (Hicks, 2019). For instance, movements such as #MeToo, #DalitLivesMatter, and #SayHerName deploy rhythmic and evocative phrasing that not only conveys an immediate political message but also fosters an affective and mnemonic impact. These hashtags function as communal literary texts, evolving as they are shared, reshaped, and recontextualized by users across different platforms and cultural settings.

The poetics of digital activism is also evident in the strategic repetition and adaptation of hashtags, which mirror oral storytelling traditions in subaltern cultures. Hashtags serve as refrains in digital discourse, much like repetitions in folk songs, protest poetry, and spoken-word performances, reinforcing collective memory and political urgency (Bonilla & Rosa, 2015). Moreover, the performative dimension of hashtag activism parallels the performative nature of resistance literature, wherein digital users engage in acts of re-narrativization by appending personal testimonies, historical references, and intertextual dialogues to a shared literary thread.

3.2. Hashtags as Digital Archives

Beyond their immediate function as tools of mobilization, hashtags serve as archival repositories of subaltern experiences, preserving and documenting histories that might otherwise be erased from institutionalized narratives. As user-generated literary records, hashtags compile a collective testimony of injustice, weaving together fragmented voices into a polyphonic textual fabric (Jackson et al., 2020). For example, #DalitVoices and #BlackLivesMatter have amassed extensive digital repositories of testimonials, poetry, visual narratives, and legal documentation, effectively constructing a grassroots historiography that challenges dominant epistemologies. This self-authored history resists the hegemony of mainstream media and state-controlled documentation, asserting the right of the marginalized to narrate their own realities.

Furthermore, the rhizomatic nature of hashtags—where a single phrase branches into interconnected sub-narratives—parallels the postmodern literary technique of hyper textuality, enabling multiple entry points into a broader discourse (Deleuze & Guattari, 1987). In this way, hashtags function as interactive literary networks, allowing readers and participants to engage, reinterpret, and expand the narrative scope of subaltern resistance.

3.3. Hashtags as a New Literary Paradigm

The rise of hashtags as literary devices signifies a shift in the relationship between activism, literature, and digital technology. They represent subaltern storytelling and allow marginalized voices to author their narratives in real-time. However, maintaining hashtags' literary and activist integrity requires ongoing engagement with digital visibility, data ethics, and platform governance. Recognizing hashtags as a distinct literary form can help ensure subaltern voices remain central in emerging literary spaces.

4. Visual Narratives and the Power of Multimedia Storytelling

In an era where digital platforms dominate contemporary discourse, visual narratives have emerged as a compelling medium for subaltern communities to reclaim agency and articulate resistance. Unlike conventional textual storytelling, which often relies on linear and linguistic structures, visual narratives employ images, videos, animations, and digital art to transcend linguistic barriers and evoke immediate emotional responses (Mirzoeff, 2015). The multisensory engagement facilitated by multimedia storytelling fosters a deeper connection between the audience and the marginalized, offering a more immersive and impactful form of digital subalternity.

4.1. Digital Storytelling: A Medium of Inclusion and Resistance

The power of multimedia storytelling lies in its ability to disrupt hegemonic discourse by centering the voices of those traditionally excluded from mainstream media and literary spaces. Platforms such as YouTube, Instagram, and TikTok have become contemporary arenas where marginalized communities document their lived realities through digital documentaries, visual essays, and performative storytelling (Losh, 2020). For instance, Indigenous activists use video storytelling to preserve oral traditions, ensuring that historical and cultural knowledge is archived for future generations (Wilson & Stewart, 2008). Similarly, Dalit activists in India leverage short films and animation to narrate historical injustices and contemporary struggles, fostering a counter-hegemonic discourse that challenges casteist narratives (Guru, 2019).

Moreover, visual storytelling fosters a participatory culture where audiences do not merely consume narratives but actively engage, comment, and share, thus co-authoring subaltern histories (Jenkins, 2006). The interactive nature of multimedia storytelling transforms digital platforms into collaborative literary spaces, where subaltern narratives evolve dynamically through audience participation and reinterpretation.

4.2. Aesthetics of Resistance: Visual Culture and Political Expression

Visual storytelling extends beyond mere representation; it serves as a political act that contests dominant ideologies, stereotypes, and erasures. The aesthetics of resistance, as seen in protest photography, street art, digital collage, and meme culture, enables the marginalized to construct alternative narratives that subvert mainstream portrayals (Taylor, 2021). For instance, viral imagery from movements such as #BlackLivesMatter, #ShaheenBaghProtests, and #IdleNoMore demonstrates how visual narratives transform into mobilizing symbols that transcend national and cultural boundaries (Bonilla & Rosa, 2015). These images encapsulate the emotional gravity of resistance, converting fleeting moments into permanent historical records that challenge systemic oppression.

Furthermore, cinematic storytelling has become an instrumental tool in articulating subaltern concerns. Independent filmmakers and grassroots content creators harness platforms such as Vimeo, Netflix, and YouTube to produce digital films that shed light on gender-based violence, racial discrimination, and forced displacement (Ginsburg, 2018). For example, documentary films such as *13th* (Ava DuVernay, 2016) and *Writing with Fire* (Rintu Thomas & Sushmit Ghosh, 2021) underscore how visual journalism and digital cinematography can foreground marginalized voices, turning digital media into a new literary canon for subaltern narratives.

4.3. The Future of Subaltern Storytelling in the Digital Age

Multimedia storytelling, combining visual culture, digital interactivity, and grassroots storytelling, is revolutionizing literary spaces for marginalized voices. It dismantles traditional hierarchies, allowing subalterns to speak and archive. However, it requires engagement with platform governance, data justice, and ethical representation. Integrating visual storytelling into digital subalternity can promote a more inclusive, participatory, and democratized literary landscape.

5. Algorithmic Gatekeeping: Challenges and Limitations of Digital Subalternity

The promise of digital platforms as egalitarian spaces for subaltern expression is increasingly undermined by algorithmic gatekeeping, a phenomenon wherein automated systems regulate visibility, engagement, and access to information. Social media algorithms, designed to maximize user engagement and corporate profit, inadvertently reinforce digital hierarchies by privileging mainstream, monetizable content over subaltern voices (Noble, 2018). The invisible curation of digital discourse by algorithms creates a new form of marginalization, wherein grassroots activism and alternative narratives struggle to gain traction within a data-driven information economy (Tufekci, 2017).

One of the key limitations of algorithmic governance is the selective amplification and suppression of content. Platforms such as Facebook, Twitter, and YouTube deploy machine-learning models that prioritize content based on user interaction metrics, often disadvantaging politically sensitive or dissenting voices (Pasquale, 2015). For instance, hashtags related to racial justice movements, Indigenous rights, and feminist activism have frequently been shadow-banned or de-ranked, limiting their organic reach (Gillespie, 2018). This algorithmic bias not only mirrors but also exacerbates historical patterns of exclusion, reinforcing the digital precarity of subaltern discourse (Benjamin, 2019).

Furthermore, algorithmic moderation mechanisms often misinterpret culturally specific expressions, dialects, and political rhetoric, leading to disproportionate content removals from marginalized communities (Bucher, 2018). Automated content filters, largely trained on Western-centric datasets, fail to account for regional linguistic nuances, thus flagging legitimate subaltern narratives as "inappropriate" or "extremist" content

(Eubanks, 2018). This technocratic form of censorship not only silences marginalized voices but also challenges the potential of social media as a democratized literary space (Gorwa, 2019).

Moreover, algorithmic bias intersects with state and corporate surveillance, posing significant ethical and political concerns for subaltern activism. Governments and private entities often collaborate with digital platforms to monitor, deplatform, or criminalize dissent, further shrinking the already limited discursive space available to marginalized groups (Zuboff, 2019). The rise of predictive analytics and AI-driven content policing increases the vulnerability of digital subalternity, turning social media into a contested terrain where freedom of expression is conditioned by opaque, profit-driven algorithms (Andrejevic, 2020).

5.1. Towards Algorithmic Justice in Digital Subalternity

While digital spaces offer unparalleled opportunities for marginalized communities to assert their narratives, the persistence of algorithmic gatekeeping necessitates urgent interventions in platform governance, data ethics, and algorithmic transparency. Advocacy for fairer digital policies, participatory AI design, and decentralized content distribution is crucial to mitigating algorithmic injustices and ensuring that digital subalternity remains a genuinely transformative literary and activist space. A critical interrogation of platform capitalism and algorithmic power will determine whether the internet remains an emancipatory domain or simply a digitized extension of historical oppression (Srnicek, 2016).

6. Beyond the Virtual: Digital Literature and Social Change

The intersection of digital literature and social change marks a transformative shift in contemporary literary spaces, where marginalized voices leverage technology to challenge dominant narratives and advocate for justice. Unlike traditional literary forms confined to print, digital literature exists as an evolving, participatory medium, allowing subaltern communities to engage with global audiences in real time (Hayles, 2008). Through blogs, interactive fiction, web-based poetry, and hypertext narratives, digital platforms have democratized literary production, dismantling gatekeeping structures that historically excluded the marginalized from the literary canon (Bolter, 2019).

A key feature of digital literature's sociopolitical impact is its ability to bridge virtual narratives with tangible activism. The rise of electronic literature, spoken-word poetry on YouTube, and web-based storytelling projects has facilitated new modes of resistance and community-building, where literature extends beyond aesthetics into direct social intervention (Murray, 2017). For instance, feminist digital memoirs, Indigenous hypertexts, and migrant storytelling archives document unheard histories, transforming personal testimonies into collective political discourse (Pressman, 2020). Such initiatives reveal how subaltern narratives, once silenced in mainstream literary circuits, find renewed agency in digital spaces, fostering intersectional dialogue and policy-level advocacy (Cayley, 2018).

Moreover, the interactive and decentralized nature of digital literature fosters a participatory culture, where readers become co-creators, engaging with marginalized perspectives through comments, hyperlinked texts, and crowdsourced storytelling projects (Rettberg, 2019). Platforms such as Wattpad, Medium, and Substack have empowered historically excluded writers to self-publish and distribute narratives without institutional validation, thereby circumventing traditional power structures (Ensslin, 2021). These digital networks not only reshape the literary economy but also cultivate alternative archives where subaltern histories, oral traditions, and counter-narratives are preserved and amplified beyond the digital sphere.

6.1. The Digital as a Catalyst for Literary Democracy

The fusion of digital literature and activism signifies a profound cultural shift, where storytelling becomes a tool for empowerment, advocacy, and systemic change. However, while digital spaces offer unprecedented access and visibility, challenges such as algorithmic suppression, digital colonialism, and platform regulation necessitate continued critical engagement with the politics of digital literary production (Jagoda, 2020). Moving beyond the virtual, the integration of digital literature into social movements, academic discourse, and policymaking is crucial to ensuring that subaltern voices are not merely heard but actively shape cultural and political landscapes.

7. Conclusion

The rise of digital subalternity underscores the transformative power of social media as an emerging literary space where marginalized voices reclaim narrative agency. Through hashtags as literature, multimedia storytelling, and participatory digital platforms, subaltern communities have transcended historical silences, embedding their lived experiences into the evolving digital literary canon (Tufekci, 2017). However, this empowerment is neither absolute nor unchallenged, as algorithmic gatekeeping, platform capitalism, and digital surveillance continue to restrict the organic growth of subaltern narratives, mirroring the hierarchies of traditional literary institutions (Noble, 2018).

Despite these challenges, digital literature fosters an alternative literary ecology, where grassroots storytelling, online activism, and interactive engagement create new pathways for cultural resistance and social transformation (Bolter, 2019). The fluidity and accessibility of digital platforms democratize literary expression, allowing subaltern communities to not only document their histories but also influence global discourses on identity, oppression, and justice (Ensslin, 2021). Moving forward, critical engagement with platform governance, data ethics, and algorithmic transparency is imperative to ensuring that digital spaces remain sites of genuine empowerment rather than extensions of existing exclusions (Zuboff, 2019).

As we navigate this shifting digital terrain, it becomes increasingly clear that social media is not merely a tool for subaltern expression but a contested literary space, where power, politics, and resistance intersect. To harness its full potential, scholars, activists, and policymakers must advocate for inclusive digital infrastructures that safeguard narrative diversity and epistemic justice. The future of digital subalternity, therefore, lies not just in amplifying marginalized voices but in dismantling the digital barriers that seek to contain them (Srnicek, 2016).

References

Andrejevic, M. (2020). *Automated Media: Algorithmic Culture and the Future of Journalism.* Routledge.

Banaji, S., & Bhat, R. (2020). *Social Media and Protest Movements: Contemporary Cases from India.* SAGE Publications.

Banet-Weiser, S. (2018). *Empowered: Popular Feminism and Popular Misogyny.* Duke University Press.

Benjamin, R. (2019). *Race After Technology: Abolitionist Tools for the New Jim Code.* Polity Press.

Bonilla, Y., & Rosa, J. (2015). "#Ferguson: Digital protest, hashtag ethnography, and the racial politics of social media in the United States." *American Ethnologist, 42*(1), 4-17.

Bruns, A., & Burgess, J. (2015). *Twitter and Society.* Peter Lang Publishing.

Bucher, T. (2018). *If...Then: Algorithmic Power and Politics.* Oxford University Press.

Couldry, N. (2010). *Why Voice Matters: Culture and Politics After Neoliberalism*. SAGE Publications.

Couldry, N., & Mejias, U. A. (2019). *The Costs of Connection: How Data is Colonizing Human Life and Appropriating It for Capitalism*. Stanford University Press.

Deleuze, G., & Guattari, F. (1987). *A Thousand Plateaus: Capitalism and Schizophrenia*. University of Minnesota Press.

Eubanks, V. (2018). *Automating Inequality: How High-Tech Tools Profile, Police, and Punish the Poor*. St. Martin's Press.

Gillespie, T. (2018). *Custodians of the Internet: Platforms, Content Moderation, and the Hidden Decisions That Shape Social Media*. Yale University Press.

Gill, R. (2021). *Mediated Activism: Political Movements and Social Media*. Polity Press.

Ginsburg, F. (2018). *Mediating Culture: Indigenous Media, Ethnographic Film, and the Politics of Representation*. University of California Press.

Gorwa, R. (2019). "What is platform governance?" *Information, Communication & Society, 22*(6), 854-871.

Guru, G. (2019). *Experience, Caste, and the Everyday Social*. Oxford University Press.

Hicks, D. (2019). *The Poetics of Digital Activism: Memory, Resistance, and Online Political Discourse*. Routledge.

Jackson, S. J., Bailey, M., & Foucault Welles, B. (2020). *#HashtagActivism: Networks of Race and Gender Justice*. MIT Press.

Jenkins, H. (2006). *Convergence Culture: Where Old and New Media Collide*. NYU Press.

Jenkins, H., Ford, S., & Green, J. (2013). *Spreadable Media: Creating Value and Meaning in a Networked Culture*. NYU Press.

Habermas, J. (1989). *The Structural Transformation of the Public Sphere: An Inquiry into a Category of Bourgeois Society*. MIT Press.

Losh, E. (2020). *Hashtag Activism: The Poetics of Resistance in Digital Culture*. Routledge.

Mirzoeff, N. (2015). *How to See the World*. Pelican Books.

Noble, S. U. (2018). *Algorithms of Oppression: How Search Engines Reinforce Racism*. NYU Press.

Rao, S. (2019). *Dalit Women's Resistance in Online Spaces: Social Media as a Platform for Advocacy and Activism*. Journal of Communication Inquiry, 43(2), 99–121.

Spivak, G. C. (1988). "Can the Subaltern Speak?" In *Marxism and the Interpretation of Culture*, ed. Nelson & Grossberg, University of Illinois Press.

Srinivasan, R. (2021). *Beyond the Valley: How Innovators around the World Are Overcoming Inequality and Creating the Technologies of Tomorrow*. MIT Press.

Taylor, D. (2021). *Performing Resistance: Digital Activism and the Aesthetics of Protest*. Oxford University Press.

Tufekci, Z. (2017). *Twitter and Tear Gas: The Power and Fragility of Networked Protest*. Yale University Press.

Wilson, S., & Stewart, P. (2008). *Indigenous Research Methods*. Fernwood Publishing.

Wilson, S. (2018). *Research Is Ceremony: Indigenous Research Methods*. Fernwood Publishing.

CHAPTER SIXTEEN

The Interplay of Margins: An Analytical Perspective on The God of Small Things

Dr. T. Ananthi,
Assistant professor of English,
Easwari Engineering College, Ramapuram, Chennai – 600089.

Abstract

This chapter, The Interplay of Margins: An Analytical Perspective on The God of Small Things, delves into Arundhati Roy's magnum opus through the lens of subaltern studies, exploring the nuanced intersection of caste, gender, and socio-political marginalization. By foregrounding the voices relegated to the periphery, the study interrogates the systemic forces that shape the destinies of the dispossessed, particularly in postcolonial Kerala. Drawing on the theoretical frameworks of Gayatri Spivak and Ranajit Guha, this analysis unravels how Roy's narrative structure subverts hegemonic discourse, amplifying the silenced narratives of the Paravan caste, transgressive women, and orphaned children. The chapter critically examines the symbolic and thematic dimensions of The God of Small Things, emphasizing the interplay between memory, trauma, and resistance within a rigidly stratified social order. Ultimately, this study situates Roy's novel within the broader discourse of subalternity, highlighting its literary significance in redefining the contours of postcolonial storytelling.

Keywords: Subaltern Studies, Caste, Gender, Marginalization, Postcolonial Literature, Trauma, Resistance, Hegemony, Memory, Arundhati Roy

The Interplay of Margins: An Analytical Perspective on *The God of Small Things*

Introduction

Arundhati Roy's *The God of Small Things* is an evocative tapestry of memory, loss, and transgression, intricately woven against the socio-political fabric of postcolonial Kerala. At its core, the novel is a profound critique of entrenched hierarchies—casteist, patriarchal, and colonial—that dictate the fates of those consigned to the peripheries of power. Through an intricate interplay of temporal fluidity and fragmented narration, Roy resurrects the voices of the marginalized—the subaltern, the dispossessed, and the silenced—who exist within the fissures of hegemonic discourse.

This chapter, *The Interplay of Margins: An Analytical Perspective on The God of Small Things*, seeks to examine the novel through the critical lens of subaltern studies, interrogating the intersections of caste oppression, gender subjugation, and socio-political marginalization. The narrative pivots around the transgressive love between Velutha, an untouchable Paravan, and Ammu, an upper-caste Syrian Christian woman—an illicit liaison that unsettles the rigid structures of caste purity and patriarchal dominance. Roy's novel, therefore, becomes a site of resistance, where the politics of love, memory, and agency challenge the normative boundaries imposed by the caste system and colonial legacies. Drawing upon the theoretical frameworks of Gayatri Spivak, Ranajit Guha, and Homi Bhabha, this study elucidates how *The God of Small Things* reconfigures the subaltern's narrative agency, thereby problematizing the very notion of history and representation. It examines the ways in which Roy deconstructs linear historiography, privileging a fragmented, cyclical temporality that mirrors the fractured identities of her subaltern protagonists. Additionally, the chapter explores the symbolic architecture of the novel, where 'small things'—whispers, glances, forbidden gestures—become acts of defiance against the grand, oppressive machinery of caste and patriarchy.

This chapter, through situating Roy's novel within the broader discourse of postcolonial and subaltern studies, seeks to foreground the literary dimensions of marginalization and resistance. It underscores how *The God of Small Things* disrupts hegemonic power structures and reclaims narrative space for those traditionally denied a voice. In doing so, it amplifies the interplay of margins—both literal and metaphorical—that shape the lives of Roy's characters, rendering the novel an enduring testament to the resilience of the silenced.

Caste and Social Hierarchies

At the heart of The God of Small Things lies the brutal realities of caste discrimination in Kerala's society. Velutha, a Dalit character, symbolizes the 'untouchable' reality. Roy exposes the violence inflicted upon marginalized communities, amplifying the structural inequalities that define India's socio-political landscape. The tragic love affair between Ammu and Velutha disrupts caste and gender norms but ultimately meets societal reprisal, underscoring the perils of defying entrenched hierarchies.

Family Dynamics and Forbidden Love

The narrative delves into the microcosm of the family, showcasing how power and oppression operate even within intimate relationships. Ammu's plight as a single mother and her yearning for love reflect the stigmatization of women who challenge patriarchal expectations. The novel uses forbidden love—whether Velutha's with Ammu or Sophie Mol's tragic demise—as a metaphor for societal transgressions and their consequences.

Colonial Legacy

Kerala's landscape, as depicted in the novel, is heavily influenced by colonial history. The Anglophilia of Baby Kochamma and the aspirations surrounding Sophie Mol epitomize the lingering presence of colonial ideologies. Roy critiques the post-colonial identity of India, dissecting the complex ways in which colonial influence persists in local culture, attitudes, and aspirations.

Narrative Techniques

Arundhati Roy's *The God of Small Things* employs an intricate and non-linear narrative structure that mirrors the fragmented realities of its marginalized protagonists. The novel's temporal fluidity, characterized by its cyclical movement between past and present, disrupts conventional historiography, reflecting the fractured consciousness of its characters. Roy's deft use of stream-of-consciousness narration immerses the reader in the interior worlds of Estha and Rahel, whose perceptions blur the boundaries between memory and reality. Additionally, her strategic use of *free indirect discourse* allows for a seamless interplay between adult retrospection and childhood innocence, reinforcing the novel's exploration of trauma and repression. Linguistically, Roy's prose oscillates between lyrical poetry and disjointed syntax, underscoring the chaotic, often suppressed, emotions of her characters. The subversion of grammatical conventions—capitalization, repetition, and neologisms—imbues the text with a rhythm that is at once haunting and rebellious, mirroring the subaltern's struggle against imposed linguistic and social structures. Moreover, the recurrent use of motifs and intertextual references—biblical allusions, postcolonial echoes, and mythological imprints—further enriches the narrative's multi-layered complexity. Through these stylistic innovations, Roy crafts a narrative that is not merely a medium of storytelling but an act of resistance against hegemonic discourse, ensuring that the voices of the subaltern resonate beyond the margins of history.

Non-linear Storytelling

Roy employs a fragmented narrative structure, intertwining past and present to reflect the disorientation of marginalized lives. This non-linear storytelling mirrors the cyclical nature of trauma and memory. Readers navigate through fractured timelines, gaining insight into the tragic inevitability of the characters' fates.

Symbolism

Roy's use of symbolism is prolific and powerful. From the Meenachal River symbolizing both life and destruction to the nuanced depiction of small things—everyday objects and moments—she underscores their profound impact on shaping the human experience. The title itself reinforces the idea that the small, often overlooked details of life hold immense significance.

Language and Style

Roy's lyrical prose combines poetry with raw emotional intensity, capturing the nuances of childhood, loss, and forbidden love. Her inventive use of language—including unique metaphors, wordplay, and repetition—creates a sensory experience that deepens readers' engagement with the narrative.

Socio-Political Commentary

Arundhati Roy's *The God of Small Things* is an incisive socio-political critique that dissects the oppressive structures embedded within caste, class, and gender hierarchies in postcolonial India. Set against the backdrop of Kerala's ostensibly progressive yet deeply stratified society, the novel unearths the insidious mechanisms of caste hegemony that persist despite ideological shifts and political upheavals. The Paravan outcaste, Velutha, epitomizes the subaltern figure—rendered invisible and disposable within the rigid framework of Brahminical patriarchy, his transgression of caste boundaries is met with brutal retribution. The narrative further exposes the hypocrisies of Communist politics, as the revolution, ostensibly advocating for the upliftment of the oppressed, ultimately reinforces the same hierarchical power dynamics it seeks to dismantle. Roy also interrogates gendered oppression, depicting Ammu's fate as emblematic of a patriarchal order that polices female agency with ruthless precision. The novel's exploration of colonial residues—manifested in the Anglophilia of the upper-caste elite and the internalization of Western moral codes—further complicates the discourse on power and subjugation. Through its layered social commentary, *The God of Small Things* becomes a searing indictment of systemic injustice, amplifying the voices of those relegated to the peripheries of history while exposing the enduring legacy of colonial and casteist violence in contemporary India.

Critique of Patriarchy

The novel provides a scathing critique of patriarchy through its portrayal of female characters who grapple with societal constraints. Ammu's ostracism, Baby Kochamma's manipulation, and Rahel's fragmented sense of self demonstrate the pervasive impact of patriarchal norms across generations.

Intersectionality

Roy brilliantly explores intersectionality—how caste, gender, and class intersect to compound oppression. For instance, Velutha faces discrimination not only as a Dalit but also as a laborer and a man who dares to love outside societal boundaries. Ammu's suffering is similarly layered, rooted in her gender, social status, and personal choices.

Resistance and Subversion

Despite its tragic undertones, the novel celebrates moments of resistance. Velutha's defiance, Rahel and Estha's bond, and Ammu's love reflect attempts to subvert societal norms and reclaim agency, even in the face of dire consequences.

Literary Significance

The God of Small Things won the Booker Prize in 1997, marking its place in global literature as a masterpiece of post-colonial fiction. Roy's portrayal of marginalized voices challenges dominant narratives and compels readers to confront uncomfortable truths about social injustice. Her ability to blend personal and political narratives has cemented the novel's legacy as a profound exploration of human existence on the periphery.

Childhood and Loss

Arundhati Roy's The God of Small Things masterfully captures the innocence, vulnerability, and fragmented experiences of childhood. The twin protagonists, Estha and Rahel, embody the emotional and psychological toll of family turmoil, societal pressures, and tragic events. Roy uses their perspective to highlight the juxtaposition of childhood wonder and the harsh realities of the adult world.

The Perspective of the Twins

The narrative oscillates between the adult and child perspectives of Estha and Rahel, creating a poignant portrayal of loss and memory. Their bond transcends verbal communication, symbolizing an unspoken understanding shaped by shared trauma. Roy's exploration of their childhood is deeply intertwined with the broader socio-political context of their lives, as the twins navigate caste-based violence, parental separation, and the death of Sophie Mol.

The Tragedy of Sophie Mol

Sophie Mol's death is a catalytic event that shatters the innocence of Estha and Rahel. Roy uses this tragedy as a lens through which to examine how societal expectations, and prejudices impose unbearable burdens on children. The narrative critiques the ways in which adult conflicts and societal norms encroach upon the haven of childhood.

Loss of Innocence

As the twins grow older, they experience a profound loss of innocence, marked by separation and a lifetime of internalized pain. Their return to Ayemenem as adults reflects their struggle to reconcile with their past and the haunting memories that continue to shape their identities.

Symbolism of Small Things

The recurring focus on "small things" in the novel is deeply tied to the experiences of Estha and Rahel. Through their eyes, small moments, objects, and gestures take on profound meaning, reflecting how children perceive and make sense of the world around them. This focus reinforces the idea that seemingly insignificant details hold immense emotional weight.

Conclusion

Arundhati Roy's The God of Small Things is an intricate tapestry that unravels the layers of marginality within Indian society. Through her evocative prose and compelling characters, Roy forces readers to reflect on the small yet monumental forces that shape lives. The novel's themes, narrative techniques, and socio-political commentary make it an enduring piece of literature that transcends boundaries and time.

References

Bhabha, Homi K. *The Location of Culture*. Routledge, 1994.

Chakrabarty, Dipesh. *Provincializing Europe: Postcolonial Thought and Historical Difference.* Princeton University Press, 2000.

Guha, Ranajit. *Elementary Aspects of Peasant Insurgency in Colonial India.* Duke University Press, 1999.

Loomba, Ania. *Colonialism/Postcolonialism.* Routledge, 2015.

Mohanty, Chandra Talpade. *Feminism Without Borders: Decolonizing Theory, Practicing Solidarity.* Duke University Press, 2003.

Roy, Arundhati. *The God of Small Things.* HarperCollins, 1997.

Said, Edward W. *Culture and Imperialism.* Knopf, 1993.

Spivak, Gayatri Chakravorty. *Can the Subaltern Speak?* Macmillan, 1988.

Romance Crippled by the Inferiority Complex of the disabled in Ruskin Bond's The Eyes Are Not Here

Dr. K. Mahendran,
Assistant Professor of English,
Career Development Centre, SRM Institute of Science and Technology,
Kattankulathur – 603 203

Abstract:
This research article investigates into the intricate portrayal of disability and tragic romance due to inferiority complex in Ruskin Bond's poignant short story, "The Eyes Are Not Here." By analysing the experiences of the disabled protagonist, this study explores how his disability and the consequential inferiority complex become entwined with themes of love, longing, and tragedy within the narrative. Drawing from disability studies, literary analysis, and romance, this article uncovers the nuanced ways in which the protagonist's disability shapes his character and relationships, ultimately illuminating the tragic romance that permeates the narrative. A visual impairment, and its intersection with his identity and sense of self. It investigates the societal stigmatization and isolation the protagonist faces due to his disability, shedding light on the enduring struggle for acceptance and connection. Furthermore, this article explores his yearning for romantic love and companionship and the challenges he encounters in pursuing such relationships. Paying a close reading of the text, supplemented by theoretical frameworks in disability studies, this research

uncovers the tragic dimension of the protagonist's romantic inclinations, revealing how his disability shapes the narrative's overall tone and emotional impact. It explores how the disability reinforces the themes of unattainable desires, isolation, and the bitter-sweet nature of human connections.

Keywords: Blind, Disability, inferiority complex, romanticism, relationships, eyes, love, nature.

Romance Crippled by the Inferiority Complex of the disabled in Ruskin Bond's *The Eyes Are Not Here*

Man is the centre of activities in the world, and it is the supremacy of man that rules not only the planet he lives on but also the heavenly bodies above. Man's mind remains a mystery even in the modern era of stupendous scientific advancements. Man's joy, sufferings and freedom are the ever-interesting subjects of intellectually rampant discussions. Man is the most intelligence and greatest living being on this earth despite any sort of his imperfections and frailties. Disability studies is one of the most significant branches of studies on man that has gathered a very keen attention in the recent times.

Disability studies is an anthropocentric approach to bring the predicaments of the disabled in spotlight and encourage the world to understand the intricate nature and functions of their psychology due to the clash of emotions out of rejections in many ways from the society. The world of the emotionally crippled due to physical and mental infirmities and their unspeakable pains and stabbing obsessions about their cursed state is yet to be deeply explored, the understanding of which takes man to the culmination of the purpose of literature itself. It challenges traditional notions of disability, advocates for social inclusion of the emotionally marginalized and promotes a more just and equitable society for all. It sheds light on the unique challenges faced by disabled individuals from diverse backgrounds.

The Eyes Are Not Here is a short story that talks of a blind man travelling by a train, who meets a girl in his compartment and tries to attract her romantically without giving any clue of his blindness, but at last he understands that the girl is also blind like him. Ruskin Bond implicitly presents the emotional shackles of a blind man and the world of blindness with miscommunications and shying away. His friendship, gratitude, romance, love, fear, doubt, sense of rejection, yearning for acceptance and love are indirectly depicted. The male ego to show himself as a very strong and perfect man to the opposite gender to attract a potential partner and his frantic attempts to get the romantic attention of girls are very evidently seen.

The narrator of Ruskin Bond's *The Eyes Are Not Here* is a blind young man, who travels to Dehra by a train. A young girl boards the train at Rohana. The narrator carefully observes the precautions being given to her by her parents, since they are very anxious about her comfort and safety. The narrator slowly acquaints with the girl and asks where she is going. She tells him that she would get down at Saharanpur, which is hardly two hours journey. The narrator is very cautious that the girl should not understand that he is blind. He goes into a deep conversation with the girl to have a memorable time with her and she also likes the way he talks and finds it interesting. The protagonist appreciates the nature that it is beautiful during this season and the girl asks him where he is heading towards. He says that he is going to Mussoorie and she is excited to tell him that he place has beautiful mountains and the nature is irresistibly engulfing anyone with a heart for beauty and peace. She says, "Oh, how lucky you are, I wish I were going to Mussoorie. I love the hills. Especially in October." He says, "Yes, this is the best time" I said, calling on my memories. "The hills are covered with wild dahlias, the sun is delicious, and at night you can sit in front of a long fire and drink a little brandy. Most of the tourists have gone and the roads are quite and almost deserted. Yes, October is the best time". (103)

The narrator compliments the girl saying that she has an interesting face. She feels delighted for such a remark and replies that many have said that she has a pretty face, but this compliment is unique. The narrator is attracted towards her sweet voice and the scented smell of her hair. When the girl is about to get down, he feels like touching her hair. But his modesty prevents him from doing so. After she gets down, another passenger enters the compartment. The narrator asks the new person whether the girl's hair is long or short. The passenger answers that he has noticed only her eyes and not her hair. He further says that she has beautiful eyes- but they are of no use, meaning that the girl is blind.

The opening scene of this short story finds the protagonist, travelling alone, sitting in a dark corner in the train coach, which is symbolic of the fact that he is emotionally alienated from the society and engulfed in the darkness of the self-imposed loneliness. He says, "I must have been sitting in a dark corner because my voice startled her." (102). Because the protagonist feels inferior to the rest of the people in the society, who are physically complete and able, he does not enjoy even the rudimentary thrilling joy and satisfaction of living in this world along with the other people. This emotional disconnection makes him withdraw himself from the collective ordinary life of his fellow human beings, but the natural attraction to a girl and the romantic inclination to be intimate with her at least verbally cannot be curtailed by any sort of physical weakness. Blind individuals are just as capable of experiencing love and forming romantic relationships as those with sight. Love is a complex and universal human emotion that transcends physical abilities, including the ability to see.

Blind people are gifted with haptic and auditory perceptions and spatial awareness. The protagonist of the story falls in love with the young and beautiful voice, the lovable manners reflected by the voice culture, tone and the pleasant feminine words of the girl. He is enchanted by the fragrance of the girl that incites his romantic imagination and hunger to share his world of affection with her. An ordinary man falls for the looks of a girl, but a blind man's way of falling in love with a girl is different, since it has nothing to do with the physical attraction.

The girl also pretends to be sighted and askes the protagonist to see out to enjoy the beauty of nature and he turns to the edge of his seat and pretends to watch the beauty of the landscape. He asks her whether she has noticed that the trees out there seem to be moving, while they seem to be still in the train compartment, and she says that it happens always.

The blind protagonist's passionate attempt to romantically connect with the girl is short-lived due to his inability to be expressive about it due to his fear and lack of confidence to be accepted and loved as he is a visually challenged person. There is a tragic friction between his natural desire to fall in love with a girl of his choice and the preventing judgement about himself that he is not a complete human being and so his proposal may be rejected. The search for an identity with the physical infirmity to be accepted in the society vs the necessity to impress his opposite gender romantically makes him a very complex person emotionally. It is comparable with any character with such a pathetically confused, suppressed and isolated individuals in black literature and subaltern literature. Oscar Wilde says, "Mutual love and respect are the fundamentals of human life" (12) but the mind of a disabled person doubts the possibilities of the reception of such fine human emotions on them due to inferiority complex. The protagonist of this story, in spite of the already existing internal tragic emotions, endeavours to communicate his passion for the girl, travelling with him, but his carefulness that she should not know that he is blind takes much of his attention and energy that he is not able to expressive about his love for the girl with an effective directness.

It is a psychological trap that the disabled are neither able to accept themselves as they are nor confident about other people's acceptance, due to the inferiority complex they have developed. The protagonist expresses his love for the girl, when he says that she has got an interesting face, but girl just stops with the thanking reply that many have told her that she is pretty, because of her doubt that she may not be accepted if he comes to know that she is blind. So, the possibility of developing the conversation into a much-awaited love is not properly made use of due to the doubts of rejection constructed by their disability.

Obsession on anything does not let the possessor to be natural, since it is a disturbance. Human mind is conditioned by the environmental and socio-political collective opinions and reactions. Any physical infirmity has its deep impact in the mind and unfortunately the mind carries the thought everywhere, which is a parasitic tragedy to the mind of the victim. The deep-rooted thought that they are inferior when compared with others normal physical state is the source of such a reluctance neither to express their love nor to accept others' love. "Pain serves as the glue that laminates the outside and inside of minority identity, ensuring that the violence enacted by society against individuals remains embedded in their psyche." (111) The tragic and self-whipping inferiority complex of the disabled does not fundamentally allow them to be natural with the normal people and so the majority of the disabled try to eclipse their physical weakness that eventually pushes them into the guilt of escaping from the truth and not fighting well to get out of it through the freedom of revealing their identity to the world and being least bothered about its reaction.

This state of mind of the disabled is fundamentally due to the societal collective belittling attitude towards them. Liam Waldron says, "Disabled persons are shown to be capable of a lot but also prevented from realising their full potential by unjust structures in society that hinder them." (355). To constantly strive towards personal freedom and fulfilment in life is the thirst of all individuals in the world. The blind narrator and the blind girl have no freedom even in the romantic world, since they are driven by such a guilt. The strange combination of feeling joyful and guilty is the painful state in the disguise of a peeping romantic encounter and joy that he can connect himself romantically with a beautiful girl. There is a very strong unexpressed sense of shame, guilt and pity at the end of this story, when the new passenger informs the protagonist that the girl is blind and so the romance of the disabled in this story is built on the compromised tragic emotions. Thus, the inferiority complex of the disabled, in this story, cripples the prospect of a mutual romance.

References

Bond, Ruskin. The Night Train at Deoli. New Delhi: Penguin Books. 1988.

Colin Barnes, Mike Oliver & Len Barton, Disability Studies Today, Polity Press 2002

Davis, L. J. (1995). Enforcing Normalcy: Disability, Deafness, and the Body. Verso Books.

Siebers, Tobin, et al. "Disability, Pain, and the Politics of Minority Identity." *Culture – Theory – Disability: Encounters between Disability Studies and Cultural Studies*, edited by Anne Waldschmidt et al., transcript Verlag, 2017, pp. 111–36. *JSTOR*,

Waldron, Liam. "Disabled Persons: Law and Love." *The Furrow*, vol. 59, no. 6, 2008, pp. 354–59. *JSTOR*, http://www.jstor.org/stable/27665764. Accessed 3 Apr. 2025.

CHAPTER EIGHTEEN

The Role of Revenge as a Form of Justice in Oppressed Communities: A Study of Baburao Bagul's Educatio

Nagendrapramoth S[1],
Ph.D. Scholar,
Annamalai University.
Dr.K.Thayalamurthy[2],
Assistant Professor of English
Government Arts and Science College
Thiruvennainallur, Villupuram.

Abstract

Revenge is a complex and deeply ingrained human response to injustice, particularly in marginalized communities where legal and social institutions fail to provide protection. Baburao Bagul's short story *Education* examines revenge as both a psychological reaction and an alternative justice mechanism within a caste-based society. This study explores the protagonist's journey from victimhood to retribution, analyzing whether his act of vengeance serves as a means of empowerment or perpetuates the cycles of violence inherent in systemic oppression. Drawing on Frantz Fanon's *The Wretched of the Earth* and B.R. Ambedkar's critique of caste hegemony, this research contextualizes the protagonist's retaliation within broader discourses of caste violence, trauma, and resistance. While revenge offers a momentary assertion of agency, it also reinforces the oppressive structures it seeks to dismantle. The study argues that Bagul presents vengeance as both a necessity and a tragedy, highlighting the failure of institutional justice and the psychological toll of caste-based violence. *Education* forces readers to confront the paradox of revenge: can it serve as justice, or does it merely sustain the very oppression it opposes? By situating Bagul's narrative within the framework of caste oppression and resistance, this research emphasizes the need for systemic transformation rather than personal retribution as the path to true justice.

Keywords: Revenge, Justice, Oppression, Caste-Based Violence, Dalit Literature, Frantz Fanon, B.R. Ambedkar, Resistance.

The Role of Revenge as a Form of Justice in Oppressed Communities: A Study of Baburao Bagul's *Education*

Revenge is a complex and deeply ingrained human response to perceived injustice, often emerging as a form of emotional, moral, and social retribution. Rooted in both instinct and cultural conditioning, revenge has been a recurring theme in literature, philosophy, and psychology, reflecting the tension between personal justice and collective morality. Across societies, revenge has been both condemned as a destructive force and celebrated as a means of restoring dignity and balance in the face of oppression.

One of the fundamental questions in the study of revenge is whether it serves as a form of justice or merely as an emotional reaction to perceived harm. Justice, in its ideal form, seeks to restore balance and ensure fairness through impartial institutions. In contrast, revenge is often personal and emotional, guided by the desire for retribution rather than reconciliation. Legal systems in modern societies are designed to replace personal revenge with institutionalized justice, yet their failures especially in marginalized communities often force individuals to take justice into their own hands.

Revenge as a response to systemic oppression has been a recurring theme in literature, particularly in narratives from marginalized communities. Often, revenge serves as a means for the oppressed to reclaim power in a world where legal and social systems fail them. Baburao Bagul's short story *Education* presents a powerful exploration of revenge as both a psychological response and a form of justice in a caste-based society.

Set in a deeply hierarchical and oppressive environment, the story highlights the protagonist's journey from victimhood to retaliation. The protagonist, shaped by violence, discrimination, and personal loss, ultimately enacts revenge against those who have wronged him and his family. However, his act of vengeance raises significant questions: Is his revenge an assertion of justice, or is it a conditioned reaction to the inescapable cycles of brutality ingrained in his society.

This research aims to examine how revenge functions as an alternative justice system when legal and social institutions fail to protect the oppressed. It explores whether the protagonist's actions serve as a restorative measure, balancing an otherwise unjust world, or if they merely continue the same patterns of violence that perpetuate systemic oppression. *Education* within the broader discourse of caste oppression, trauma, and resistance, this study will assess how Bagul portrays revenge as a double-edged sword a moment of personal agency that simultaneously reinforces a violent societal structure.

Baburao Bagul's short story *Education* offers a profound commentary on caste-based oppression, where revenge emerges not just as an emotional response but as a means of resistance against systemic injustice. The story portrays how caste-based discrimination, institutional failures, and personal trauma shape the protagonist's perception of justice, ultimately leading him to seek revenge. This act of vengeance, however, is not merely an individual reaction but a deeply ingrained response to a social structure that denies justice to the oppressed.

In *Education*, caste-based oppression manifests through various forms of violence both physical and psychological. The protagonist, growing up in a brutal and exploitative social order, experiences oppression first hand. His family suffers at the hands of those in power, particularly his brother-in-law, who abuses his sister and mother. The failure of legal and social institutions to intervene reinforces the protagonist's belief that justice cannot be obtained through official channels.

Bagul's narrative aligns with the broader experience of Dalit communities, who have historically faced systemic exclusion from legal and moral justice. When society denies justice to the marginalized, revenge often becomes the only available recourse. The protagonist's retaliation, therefore, is not merely personal but also a symbolic act against the caste system that has perpetuated his suffering.

The protagonist's act of revenge is fuelled by personal grief and unresolved trauma. The brutalization of his sister and mother leaves him with deep psychological scars, shaping his worldview around violence as both a cause and consequence of oppression. His decision to retaliate with a hockey stick, a symbol of his suppressed rage, is not just an impulsive reaction but an assertion of his agency in a world that denies him power.

Frantz Fanon, in *The Wretched of the Earth*, discusses how colonial and caste-based oppression dehumanizes individuals, leading them to see violence as a means of reclaiming lost dignity. Similarly, in Education, the protagonist's vengeance is his way of breaking free from victimhood, albeit through the same violent means that oppressed him.

A key question that emerges is whether the protagonist's revenge is an act of justice or a product of social conditioning. In a society where caste-based hierarchy enforces a cycle of violence, revenge does not necessarily break the system but rather reinforces it by normalizing brutality as a response. His retaliation is an attempt to restore balance in an unjust world, echoing Ambedkar's ideas on resistance against caste hegemony. On the other hand, it also raises the moral dilemma of whether violence, even against the oppressor, leads to true liberation or simply perpetuates oppression in a new form.

Bagul's story presents revenge as both a necessity and a tragedy. While it gives the protagonist a sense of control, it also highlights the grim reality that justice remains inaccessible to the oppressed unless they take matters into their own hands. The story ultimately challenges the reader to consider whether revenge can ever lead to real justice, or if it only reinforces the same structures of oppression that it seeks to dismantle.

This study explores the relationship between education and caste-based violence, emphasizing that while revenge empowers the protagonist, it also signifies a broader societal failure to safeguard its most marginalized individuals. The cycle of violence continues, suggesting that true justice can only be achieved by dismantling the oppressive structures themselves, rather than through individual acts of retaliation.

Baburao Bagul's *Education* presents revenge as a complex and paradoxical response to caste-based oppression. The protagonist's journey highlights the tension between revenge as a form of empowerment and its potential to lead to self-destruction. While vengeance grants him a sense of agency in a world that has systematically oppressed him, it also entraps him in a cycle of violence that ultimately reinforces the very system he seeks to resist.

Revenge can be an assertion of agency in a society that denies justice of marginalized communities. The protagonist of Education is a victim of brutal caste-based violence, witnessing his sister's suffering and his mother's humiliation at the hands of a dominant figure. His act of violence against his oppressor is, in many ways, a reclamation of power.

"His mother's eyes—tired, weary, humiliated—haunted him in the dark. He could hear his sister's sobs even in silence. He clenched his fists, his body burning with an unbearable rage" (52).

This captures how trauma and powerlessness fuel his desire for vengeance, shaping his sense of justice. He shifts from being a passive sufferer to an active agent in his fate. He refuses to accept the injustices imposed on him, taking matters into his own hands when legal and social institutions fail him. Revenge becomes a way for the protagonist to free himself from the fear and helplessness imposed by an oppressive system. His violent act gives him a sense of control over his destiny, something he has been denied throughout his life.

Frantz Fanon, in *The Wretched of the Earth*, argues that for the oppressed, violence can be a means of self-actualization. In a world where subjugation is the norm, revenge serves as a radical act of defiance, a way to challenge the structures that maintain power imbalances (85). While revenge appears empowering in the moment, it also traps the protagonist in an endless cycle of violence. Instead of liberating him, his actions lead to further suffering and alienation.

The protagonist risks replicating the very cruelty that was inflicted upon him. Instead of dismantling the oppressive system, his revenge reinforces violence as the only language of justice, ensuring that the next generation will continue to suffer. The story hints at the protagonist's likely imprisonment, suggesting that his moment of empowerment comes at the cost of his future. The institutions that failed to protect him will still punish him, reinforcing that justice remains inaccessible to the oppressed. Bagul emphasizes this, writing, "The blood on his hands was warm, but so was the knowledge that the police would come for him soon" (58).

Psychological Toll: Though the protagonist takes revenge, his anger and trauma do not disappear. Violence may give him temporary relief, but it does not undo his suffering. Instead, it deepens his wounds, making healing impossible.

Anand Patil, a literary critic on Dalit literature, suggests that Dalit narratives often portray revenge as both cathartic and futile, showing how the oppressed are often left with no recourse but retaliation, yet this act does not change the system (112). This aligns with the protagonist's fate in *Education* explains his actions do not free him but instead solidify his place as both victim and aggressor.

The story forces us to question whether revenge is truly a form of justice or merely a symptom of a broken system. If justice were accessible, would the protagonist have needed to take matters into his own hands. The fact that revenge is his only option underscores the failure of legal and social institutions to protect marginalized individuals.

The protagonist's journey suggests that while revenge may feel like justice in the short term, it does not bring long-term change. True empowerment, Bagul seems to suggest, comes not from personal vengeance but from systemic transformation dismantling the structures that necessitate revenge in the first place.

Revenge in *Education* is both empowering and self-destructive. It allows the protagonist to momentarily seize control, but it does not offer him a path forward. His act of vengeance exposes the deep flaws of the social system, yet it does not change them. Instead, it leaves him trapped, showing that revenge, while personally satisfying, is not a sustainable solution to oppression.

Bagul's story challenges the reader to reflect on the true meaning of justice. If revenge is the only form of justice available to the oppressed, then the real question is not whether revenge leads to empowerment or destruction, but rather why society forces the marginalized to seek justice through violence in the first place.

Baburao Bagul's short story *Education* is a powerful critique of how legal and social institutions fail oppressed individuals, leaving them with no option but to seek justice through violent means. The protagonist, a young Dalit boy, experiences systemic oppression first hand, witnessing the humiliation and suffering of his family at the hands of upper-caste individuals. When legal and societal structures refuse to intervene, his only recourse becomes an act of personal revenge. This analysis explores how the institutional failures in the story push marginalized individuals toward violence, substantiating the argument with textual evidence and critical perspectives.

The protagonist's family, like many others from oppressed communities, has no access to justice because the legal system is designed to uphold caste hierarchies rather than protect the marginalized. When his sister is assaulted, no authorities intervene, and no justice is served.

"The law was there, but for whom? Not for those like him. The policeman had laughed when his mother pleaded for justice, his eyes mocking their helplessness" (47).

This passage exposes how the very institutions meant to uphold justice instead reinforce oppression. The protagonist understands that appealing to the legal system is futile, as it is controlled by the same upper-caste individuals who exploit them. This reality is reflective of the broader historical context in India, where Dalits have often been denied legal recourse due to caste biases in law enforcement and the judiciary.

Education also examines how deeply embedded social structures beyond legal inaction it sustains against oppression and hinder meaningful challenges. The protagonist's family faces humiliation and subjugation not just from individuals but from an entire system that normalizes their suffering.

"His mother had worked for them her whole life, bent double in servitude. Yet, when she asked for justice, they called her impudent, laughed in her face, and sent her away with nothing but curses." (49).

This illustrates that the social system does not merely fail to provide justice, it actively punishes those who seek it. The protagonist's mother, who represents countless Dalit women subjected to generational exploitation, is dismissed and ridiculed instead of being heard. The protagonist, witnessing this, realizes that the world offers no justice for people like him unless he takes it by force. with no access to legal recourse and no social support, the protagonist internalizes violence as the only possible response to the oppression he and his family suffer. His decision to take revenge is not merely a personal one but a reflection of a broken system that leaves him with no alternative.

"There was no law for him, no justice, only the weight of his mother's tears and his sister's silence. He picked up the sickle—if the world would not grant him justice, he would carve it out himself." (56).

This act of vengeance is not born out of mere anger but out of necessity as a result of the systemic barriers that prevent justice through non-violent means. It echoes the argument made by Frantz Fanon in *The Wretched of the Earth*,

"When the legal order itself becomes the instrument of oppression, the only recourse for the oppressed is violence; not as a choice, but as the only language the oppressor understands" (89).

Fanon's insight helps contextualize the protagonist's actions as part of a broader historical pattern where oppressed individuals and communities resort to violent resistance when all other means of justice are denied to them.

Bagul's *Education* provides a harrowing exploration of how legal and social systems fail the oppressed, forcing them into cycles of violence as a desperate form of justice. The protagonist's journey demonstrates that his act of revenge is not a mere personal vendetta but a tragic necessity imposed by a society that refuses to protect him. His actions, while momentarily empowering, do not lead to real justice or systemic change—only further alienation and suffering.

As Fanon argues, the oppressed do not turn to violence because they desire it, but because the world gives them no other path. The story, in this way, serves as an indictment of the structures that uphold injustice and a call to dismantle these systems so that justice does not have to be sought through bloodshed.

This research incorporates Frantz Fanon's *The Wretched of the Earth* as a critical framework for analysing revenge as a psychological and socio-political response to systemic violence. Fanon's argument that violence emerges as an inevitable consequence of colonization and oppression is particularly relevant in examining Education. It contextualizes the protagonist's revenge not as a mere act of individual defiance but as part of a larger historical pattern wherein oppressed communities, denied justice, resort to extra-legal means of retribution. Through this lens, Education serves as a case study in how systemic oppression forces individuals to equate revenge with justice, highlighting the tragic consequences of such a reality.

This research critically examines whether Baburao Bagul's *Education* presents revenge as a necessary evil, an act of justice, or a tragic consequence of systemic oppression. The protagonist's journey underscores the limitations of conventional legal and social structures in providing justice for marginalized individuals, forcing them to seek alternative means of retribution. However, this study also interrogates whether revenge functions as a genuine mechanism for empowerment or merely reinforces the cycle of violence that sustains caste-based oppression. While the protagonist's act of vengeance momentarily grants him a sense of agency, it ultimately does not alter the power structures that oppress him. Instead, it places him in a precarious position where he is simultaneously liberated from his victimhood yet entrapped within the very system he sought to resist.

The broader implications of this study suggest that revenge, as depicted in Education, operates as both a form of resistance and a symptom of a broken justice system. Rather than serving as a solution, vengeance in oppressed communities often emerges as a desperate response to structural violence, one that ultimately fails to dismantle the systems of oppression. Bagul's narrative compels readers to question whether justice should be sought through personal retaliation or through collective, systemic transformation. This research highlights the urgent need to explore alternative avenues for justice that do not rely on the perpetuation of violence, advocating for structural reforms that address the root causes of oppression rather than their manifestations in acts of revenge.

REFERENCE:

Bagul, Baburao. "Education." *Death is Getting Cheaper*. Translated by Dr. Kishor N. Ingole and Dr. Nirmala S. Padmavat, Notion Press, 2023.

Ambedkar, B.R. *Annihilation of Caste*. Navayana Publishing, 2014.

Fanon, Frantz. *The Wretched of the Earth*. Translated by Richard Philcox, Grove Press, 2004.

Patil, Anand. *Dalit Literature and Resistance*. Oxford University Press, 2015.

CHAPTER NINETEEN

Cartographies of Exclusion: Spatial Segregation and the Dalit Experience in My Father Balaiah

Dr.M.Ratchagar[1],
Lecturer in English,
Government Polytechnic College,
Kooduveli, Tamil Nadu, India.
Mrs. S. Kalaiselvi [2],
Lecturer in English,
Government Polytechnic College,
Villupuram,Tamil Nadu, India.

Abstract

This article explores spatial segregation and caste-based exclusion in Y. B. Satyanarayana's *My Father Balaiah* through the lens of cartography and spatial theory. It argues that the physical and symbolic separation of Dalit communities in postcolonial India constitutes a lived cartography of marginality. Drawing on the memoir as a primary source, alongside works by scholars such as Gopal Guru, B. R. Ambedkar, and Henri Lefebvre, the article examines how geography intersects with caste to produce a landscape of exclusion that is both material and ideological.

Keywords:

Dalit autobiography; spatial exclusion; caste geography; social marginality; ritual segregation.

Cartographies of Exclusion: Spatial Segregation and the Dalit Experience in My Father Balaiah

Dalit autobiographies are not merely personal narratives; they are also socio-political cartographies, tracing the geography of exclusion etched into the Indian landscape. Y. B. Satyanarayana's *My Father Balaiah* (2011) serves as a poignant exemplar of this, documenting the spatial and social alienation experienced by the Madiga caste. The narrative portrays a family navigating displacement, humiliation, and eventual self-assertion, while continually confronting the invisible yet pervasive borders imposed by caste hierarchies.

The intersection of space and caste in India is not merely a sociological curiosity—it is a lived, daily experience that structures the lives of millions. Y. B. Satyanarayana's autobiographical narrative *My Father Balaiah* (2011) is an evocative exploration of how caste oppression operates through spatial arrangements—both rural and urban—reproducing hierarchies of purity, pollution, and exclusion. This essay critically investigates the spatial implications of caste as portrayed in the text, using theoretical frameworks from Henri Lefebvre, Gopal Guru, and B. R. Ambedkar to ground its argument. This theoretical insight finds real expression in *My Father Balaiah*. Satyanarayana recounts: "Our hamlet of Madiga huts was separated from the main village by a stretch of open land, as though our presence might pollute the air itself" (Satyanarayana 3). This is not merely physical separation but a ritualized geography, where spatial design reinforces caste codes.

Dr. B. R. Ambedkar, a pioneering thinker on caste and space, observed that untouchability operates through mechanisms of enforced distance. In *Annihilation of Caste*, he writes: "Caste is not merely a division of labour; it is also a division of labourers" (Ambedkar). This division is visual and spatial—who lives where, who draws water from which well, and who enters which door. In *My Father Balaiah*, the author recalls incidents from school where he was made to sit separately and denied water: "I was told to bring my own tumbler. If I forgot it, I went thirsty" (Satyanarayana 44). This spatial rule—of keeping the Dalit body physically apart—reveals how caste translates into bodily geography. The body itself becomes a site of spatial control.

Gopal Guru's argument that Dalits are excluded from the moral geography of the Indian nation becomes particularly compelling in this context. In his essay "Dalits from Margin to Margin," he asserts that the caste system deprives Dalits of civic and moral inclusion in national space. According to Guru, "the marginalization of Dalits is not merely social or economic—it is also spatial and epistemic" (Guru 114). *My Father Balaiah* reflects this when Satyanarayana notes how his family, despite relocating to an urban center like Secunderabad, was still forced into liminal spaces near the railway tracks and drainage systems—urban ghettos echoing rural untouchability. "The land may have been different, but the distance remained the same," he reflects (Satyanarayana 87). Thus, modernity does not automatically translate to spatial justice for Dalits.

Urban space, often viewed as liberating, is shown in the memoir to be another site of caste-coded navigation. The narrator's family shifts locations multiple times, but space continues to be denied, negotiated, and transgressed. The narrator observes: "Our movements from village to town didn't mean we had escaped caste. It travelled with us, marked us, followed us into every corner" (Satyanarayana 92).This aligns with D. R. Nagaraj's insight that caste is not just rural; it is "deeply embedded even in the most 'modern' institutions" (Nagaraj 48). The continuity of spatial discrimination in city life undermines the myth of urbanity as a caste-neutral zone.Y. B. Satyanarayana's *My Father Balaiah* provides a profoundly personal yet politically significant narrative that reveals how caste structures Indian space at every level—from village huts to urban shanties, from schoolrooms to water sources. Grounded in theoretical insights from Lefebvre, Ambedkar, and Gopal Guru, the memoir underscores the spatiality of caste as both a lived reality and a theoretical framework for understanding the geography of inequality. It challenges us to rethink spatial justice as an essential part of the Dalit struggle for dignity and equality.

Geographies are not merely physical terrains; they are socio-political terrains etched with power, privilege, and exclusion. In the Indian context, marginality is often spatial, rooted in the centuries-old caste system that locates Dalit communities on the fringes—geographically, socially, and symbolically. Y. B. Satyanarayana's *My Father Balaiah* (2011) offers a rich autobiographical narrative that uncovers how these geographies of marginality operate in both rural and urban contexts. This essay examines the spatial dimensions of caste marginalization in the text and argues that *My Father Balaiah* functions as a counter-cartography—a reclaiming of space, voice, and dignity.

In *My Father Balaiah*, spatial marginality begins in the village. The Madiga community to which the narrator belongs is consigned to the

"Madiga wada"—a separate hamlet on the edge of the village, far removed from the homes of upper-caste communities. Satyanarayana writes, "We lived in a row of mud huts, placed far away from the main part of the village... like we were not supposed to exist in the same landscape" (Satyanarayana 3). This spatial exclusion reflects the structural hierarchy that denies Dalits access to resources, dignity, and belonging. The separation is not only physical but ritualistic and symbolic. B. R. Ambedkar emphasized that caste operates through "graded inequality," where spatial separation reinforces the ideology of pollution and purity (*Annihilation of Caste*). By being physically relegated to peripheral spaces, Dalits are marked as socially inferior and morally suspect.

The narrative captures how the built environment reproduces caste hierarchies through spatial practices. Satyanarayana recounts how, as a child, he could not drink water from the school tap and had to bring his own tumbler. "If I forgot it, I went thirsty. Even water had to obey caste boundaries" (Satyanarayana 44). This simple act underscores how space becomes a technology of oppression, a way of policing bodies and maintaining untouchability.

Scholar Gopal Guru refers to this as the "spatial aesthetics of humiliation"—spaces designed and inhabited in ways that continually remind Dalits of their place in the hierarchy (Guru 2000). Whether it is the location of homes, access to water, or seating in classrooms, these geographies are saturated with discrimination.

The move from village to city does not dismantle the architecture of exclusion. When Balaiah moves his family to Secunderabad, they inhabit temporary quarters near the railway lines—spaces of transience, instability, and vulnerability. Satyanarayana observes: "We lived on land that belonged to someone else. It was clear we were only temporary dwellers—allowed to exist, but not to belong" (Satyanarayana 87). Urban landscapes, though spatially dense and seemingly anonymous, reproduce marginality through slums, ghettos, and infrastructure that mark certain populations as other. Henri Lefebvre's theory in *The Production of Space* affirms that "every society produces a space, its own space," reflecting the political and economic structures of that society (Lefebvre 31). In India, even the cosmopolitan spaces of cities are complicit in reproducing caste-based marginality. Dalit families find themselves in unplanned, undesirable locations, often without legal claim to land or security.

Despite these geographies of exclusion, *My Father Balaiah* is also a narrative of resistance. Balaiah's insistence on educating his children becomes a symbolic re-mapping—an attempt to move across forbidden spaces, from the periphery to the center. Education, in this context, is not just a means of employment but a spatial assertion, a way of occupying institutions and ideologies previously barred to Dalits. Satyanarayana later becomes a professor, entering the academic space as a Dalit subject who reclaims voice and authority. This shift reflects what D. R. Nagaraj identifies as the "transition from humiliation to self-respect" (Nagaraj 18). The memoir thus does not simply record marginality—it redraws the map, asserting Dalit presence in places of exclusion.

My Father Balaiah offers a compelling geography of marginality, revealing how caste determines where people live, where they are allowed to go, and what they are allowed to become. Drawing on theoretical perspectives from Ambedkar, Lefebvre, Guru, and Nagaraj, the memoir can be read as a spatial critique of the Indian caste system. Yet, it is also a document of transformation, in which the cartography of exclusion is rewritten by the courage and resilience of those who refuse to remain invisible.

The deeply entrenched caste system in India manifests not only in social relations and economic hierarchies but also in the very organization of space. The boundary that separates the so-called "untouchables" from upper castes is often spatially literal—seen in segregated housing, restricted access to resources, and the everyday geography of exclusion. Y. B. Satyanarayana's *My Father Balaiah* (2011) powerfully narrates how these spatial borders uphold social boundaries, shaping the lived experience of Dalits. This essay examines the spatial logic of caste-based segregation, drawing from critical theorists like B. R. Ambedkar, Gopal Guru, and Henri Lefebvre, and inferring how the physical demarcations around Dalit lives reflect larger ideological and cultural boundaries.

One of the clearest illustrations of spatial boundary enforcing caste status appears early in *My Father Balaiah*. Satyanarayana writes, "Our Madiga wada was a cluster of huts away from the main village. We were separated by distance and by intent" (Satyanarayana 3). This physical separation is not accidental; it is systematically designed to enforce the doctrine of purity and pollution. Henri Lefebvre's idea in *The Production of Space* that "space is not a passive locus but an active site of social relations" (Lefebvre 68) helps frame the Dalit habitation not as peripheral but as deliberately constructed zones of exclusion. These borders are embedded in ritual and daily life and act as spatial reminders of one's place in the social hierarchy.

B. R. Ambedkar famously stated, "Untouchability is not only a social problem; it is a problem of physical contact" (*Annihilation of Caste*). The spatial borders described in *My Father Balaiah* are, thus, not only geographical but also bodily. At school, the narrator recounts: "I was told not to touch the water pot. I had to bring my own tumbler. Even water obeyed caste rules" (Satyanarayana 44). The restriction of space around the Dalit child's body creates a zone of avoidance, enforcing the idea that Dalit presence is defiling. Gopal Guru describes this as "the ontological distancing of the Dalit body" (Guru 2000), wherein the space surrounding Dalits becomes charged with social stigma. The social boundary is literally mapped onto the body, and spatial distancing becomes a mode of disciplining that body.

While the family's move from village to city promises hope, it does not dismantle these entrenched boundaries. In Secunderabad, they reside near the railway lines in temporary housing. Satyanarayana observes: "Though we were in the city, we were still on the edge, living on borrowed land, excluded from the city's core" (Satyanarayana 88). The geography of marginality reconstitutes itself, adapting to modern urban structures.

Dalit urban housing, as Gyan Prakash notes, often "emerges not from planning but from exclusion from planning" (Prakash 2002). The borders are now marked by infrastructure, economic neglect, and legal precarity, but they continue to serve the same function: to segregate and disempower. Social boundaries extend into institutions such as schools, offices, and bureaucracies. Satyanarayana recalls the internalized shame and fear of entering official buildings or public offices, writing, "We didn't know how to stand, where to sit, or whether to even speak inside those walls" (Satyanarayana 102). These are symbolic spatial borders—walls that keep Dalits out not by law but by habit, humiliation, and historic exclusion. Here again, Lefebvre's theory becomes relevant. The "representational space," or how space is experienced and imbued with meaning, becomes hostile for Dalit subjects. These spaces reject Dalit presence, subtly but forcefully, reinforcing social boundaries. In addition to documenting pain and humiliation, the text performs a cartography of resistance—a conscious remapping of social space through acts of dignity, mobility, and assertion. This essay explores how Satyanarayana's memoir charts the trajectory of resistance and reclamation by a Dalit family in a casteist society, while drawing upon critical perspectives from B. R. Ambedkar, Gopal Guru, and D. R. Nagaraj.

One of the most powerful forms of resistance in *My Father Balaiah* is the pursuit of education, often denied to Dalit communities. Balaiah, the narrator's father, insists on sending his children to school despite his own lack of formal education. He declares, "Education alone can take us out of this mud" (Satyanarayana 48). The metaphor of "mud" as symbolic of Dalit degradation is crucial—education becomes the route out of this stuck geography, a means of redrawing the family's spatial and social map.

B. R. Ambedkar advocated education as the first principle of emancipation: "Cultivate the mind. It is the mind that makes the body and the man" (*Annihilation of Caste*). In the text, Balaiah enacts this philosophy in practice. His vision lays the groundwork for epistemic resistance, a term Gopal Guru uses to describe how Dalits "create alternative modes of knowledge against caste-based silencing" (Guru and Sarukkai 2012).

The memoir documents how the family gradually enters institutional spaces that were historically denied to them—schools, universities, offices. Y. B. Satyanarayana becomes a professor, and his presence in academia represents a symbolic conquest of space. He writes, "When I sat behind the teacher's desk for the first time, I felt the walls of centuries cracking" (Satyanarayana 143). This moment is a profound act of reclamation, not only of physical space but also of voice and authority. Henri Lefebvre's theory that space is "not a thing but a set of relations" (*The Production of Space* 86) applies here: Satyanarayana redefines spatial relations by occupying spaces that once excluded people like him. His professional ascent is not just social mobility—it is spatial counterinsurgency, reclaiming caste-coded geographies and redefining their meaning. By documenting his life story and that of his father, Satyanarayana engages in what D. R. Nagaraj calls the "aesthetics of assertion"—a form of storytelling that challenges the dominant cultural narrative (Nagaraj 18). Dalit autobiography, particularly *My Father Balaiah*, becomes a map of memory—an alternative archive that records the lived geography of oppression and defiance.

Satyanarayana's recollections are not linear but spatial; they move from village to city, from hut to school, from railway colony to university. These movements resist the fixity of caste identity. "We never stopped moving—not because we were restless, but because the world didn't want us to settle," he writes (Satyanarayana 91). Here, movement itself becomes resistance against stasis, a refusal to be spatially and socially confined. The memoir also resists linguistic erasure by telling a Dalit story in English, a language often associated with upper-caste elites. By doing so, Satyanarayana reclaims the medium of national and global discourse. Gopal Guru and Sundar Sarukkai assert that Dalits must "not only occupy space but produce knowledge within it" (Guru and Sarukkai 2012). *My Father Balaiah* is precisely this—a knowledge-project that maps resistance through narrative. Moreover, the very act of naming the autobiography after his father is an act of honor and reclamation of dignity. It subverts generations of invisibility and silence by positioning a Madiga railway worker as a figure of moral, cultural, and intellectual significance.

My Father Balaiah is not only an autobiographical account but also a spatial document—a cartography of exclusion and resistance. It illustrates how caste manifests geographically, reinforcing the margins as a physical and ideological construct. Yet, in narrating this exclusion, Satyanarayana reclaims space, challenging the boundaries that sought to contain him. In doing so, he contributes to an emergent Dalit spatial imagination that refuses to remain on the periphery.

Works Cited

Ambedkar, B. R. *Annihilation of Caste*. Navayana, 2014.

Guru, Gopal. "Dalits from Margin to Margin." *India International Centre Quarterly*, vol. 27, no. 2, 2000, pp. 111–122.

Guru, Gopal, and Sundar Sarukkai. *The Cracked Mirror: An Indian Debate on Experience and Theory*. Oxford University Press, 2012.

Lefebvre, Henri. *The Production of Space*. Translated by Donald Nicholson-Smith, Blackwell, 1991.

Nagaraj, D. R. *The Flaming Feet and Other Essays: The Dalit Movement in India*. Edited by Prithvi Datta Chandra Shobhi, Permanent Black, 2010.

Prakash, Gyan. *The Urban Turn. Sarai Reader 02: The Cities of Everyday Life*, Centre for the Study of Developing Societies, 2002.

Satyanarayana, Y. B. *My Father Balaiah*. HarperCollins India, 2011.

CHAPTER TWENTY

Echoes from the Edge: An Ecocritical Reading of Peripheral Survival in 21st Century India

Dr. Kanika Godara,
Assistant Professor,
Galgotias University.

Abstract:

In 21st-century India, peripheral geographies—spanning rural wastelands, urban slums, and indigenous lands—serve as crucibles where marginalized voices confront ecological devastation and social exclusion. This chapter, "Echoes from the Edge: An Ecocritical Reading of Peripheral Survival in 21st Century India," employs ecocriticism to explore how contemporary Indian literature reimagines these margins as sites of resilience and resistance. Focusing on Arundhati Roy's *The Ministry of Utmost Happiness*, Hansda Sowvendra Shekhar's *The Adivasi Will Not Dance*, and Dalit poetry by Meena Kandasamy and Yogesh Maitreya, the study examines how narrative reclamation transforms degraded landscapes—graveyards, mined forests, and polluted rivers—into spaces of survival and identity. These works reveal the interplay between ecological collapse and social marginality, foregrounding ecological consciousness as a lens through which peripheral communities assert agency against slow violence. In Roy's novel, a transgender protagonist reclaims a graveyard as a refuge, embodying resilience amidst urban decay. Shekhar's Adivasi characters resist cultural and environmental erasure, their identity tied to the land they refuse to surrender. This chapter argues that these marginalized voices challenge hegemonic narratives of progress, which often equate development with ecological and human displacement. Instead, they offer a vision of coexistence rooted in interdependence with the non-human world, highlighting literature's capacity for narrative reclamation. By amplifying echoes from India's edges, these texts underscore the vitality of peripheral geographies as more than mere margins—they are dynamic terrains where ecological consciousness and cultural defiance converge. Through this ecocritical analysis, the chapter contributes to an interdisciplinary dialogue on how literature unveils the tenacity of peripheral life, redefining survival as both an ecological and existential act in the face of systemic erasure.

Keywords: Resilience, Ecocriticism, Peripheral Geographies, Marginalized Voices and, Resistance

Echoes from the Edge: An Ecocritical Reading of Peripheral Survival in 21st Century India

Introduction

In 21st-century India, environmental crises—driven by climate change, industrial exploitation, deforestation, and urban expansion—disproportionately affect marginalized communities. Rural wastelands, urban slums, and indigenous territories, often sidelined in development narratives, are both ecological frontiers and sociopolitical margins. Yet, in contemporary Indian literature, these "sacrificial zones" emerge as spaces of resilience and resistance.

This paper offers an ecocritical reading of Arundhati Roy's *The Ministry of Utmost Happiness*, Hansda Sowvendra Shekhar's *The Adivasi Will Not Dance*, and selected Dalit poetry by Meena Kandasamy and Yogesh Maitreya. These works reframe degraded and liminal spaces as sites of agency, where survival itself becomes a form of defiance. Drawing on Rob Nixon's concept of "slow violence," the study highlights how environmental harm intersects with caste, class, gender, and ethnicity in India.

Through close textual analysis and a framework combining ecocriticism, postcolonial, and subaltern studies, the paper explores how literature reclaims silenced environmental histories and imagines new possibilities for coexistence amid ecological precarity.

Peripheral Landscapes as Sites of Survival and Identity
Conceptualizing the Edge

In Indian literature, the "periphery" serves not only as a spatial marker but as a metaphor for exclusion, resistance, and transformation. Traditionally positioned against the urban, privileged center, the periphery represents communities marginalized by caste, class, gender, and ethnicity. Contemporary Indian literature challenges this binary by depicting these spaces as sites of resilience and identity.

In *The Ministry of Utmost Happiness*, Arundhati Roy explores the urban periphery through Anjum, a hijra who builds a sanctuary in a Delhi graveyard—"She lived in the graveyard like a tree lives inside the earth" (Roy 3). This graveyard becomes a counter-space to dominant narratives of nationalism and urban order. Similarly, Hansda Sowvendra Shekhar's *The Adivasi Will Not Dance* brings the rural and tribal periphery to the forefront, exposing systemic exploitation and ecological violence. The narrator's refusal to perform—"I will not dance... I will not sing and I will not entertain" (Shekhar 175)—asserts cultural resistance to state-driven commodification of Adivasi identity.

These texts underscore how environmental degradation is intertwined with social marginalization. Rob Nixon's concept of "slow violence," which unfolds "gradually and out of sight" and is "dispersed across time and space" (Nixon 2), is crucial for understanding how pollution, displacement, and deforestation impact those already living on the margins of both geography and power.

The Role of Space and Place

Place-making becomes an act of resistance in these peripheral narratives. By reclaiming spaces historically marked by neglect or abjection—graveyards, mining zones, polluted rivers—marginalized characters affirm their belonging and agency. These landscapes are not inert backdrops but active participants in the struggle for survival and identity. In Roy's novel, the graveyard is not just a shelter but a site of transformation where Anjum, along with other social outcasts, constructs an alternative community that challenges dominant notions of purity, progress, and productivity. "It was as though the place itself—its history, its bones—had decided to gather them all in," Roy writes, underscoring the graveyard's role as a generative rather than morbid space (Roy 27).

In Shekhar's short stories, place is similarly imbued with ancestral and spiritual significance. The forests and rivers are not merely resources but extensions of Adivasi identity and memory. The dispossession of these lands amounts to a cultural and existential erasure, making the act of remaining—of not migrating or surrendering—an ecological and political stance. As one character states, "This is not just soil... it is our mother, our god" (Shekhar 89).

Thus, the periphery in these texts is neither a void nor a victim. It is a vibrant landscape where spatial exclusion is met with narrative reclamation, and where identity is forged not in spite of ecological devastation, but through a deeply embodied and affective relationship with place. These works compel a rethinking of environmental discourse in India, urging us to consider how the geographies of survival are shaped by, and in turn shape, the politics of belonging and resistance.

Arundhati Roy's *The Ministry of Utmost Happiness*: Graveyard as Refuge

Spatial Politics of the Graveyard

In *The Ministry of Utmost Happiness*, Arundhati Roy transforms the graveyard—traditionally a space associated with death and abandonment—into a vibrant sanctuary that resists dominant narratives of development and exclusion. Situated on the margins of Delhi, the graveyard becomes a liminal space that blurs the boundaries between life and death, sacred and profane, center and periphery. By turning this neglected space into a communal home, Roy subverts the spatial politics of urban planning, where "usable" land is often measured by its potential for profit, not its capacity for healing and inclusion.

Roy introduces the graveyard early in the novel as a place where Anjum, a hijra protagonist, chooses to live after experiencing state and social rejection. "She lived in the graveyard like a tree lives inside the earth. Effortlessly. Rootedly" (Roy 3). This imagery suggests not just survival but a symbiotic relationship with the earth, framing the graveyard as a site of organic resilience. In this act of spatial reclamation, Anjum disrupts the sanitized, exclusionary logic of modern urbanism. The graveyard thus becomes what Michel Foucault might call a "heterotopia"—a counter-site that challenges the norms and structures of the mainstream city (Foucault 24).

Transgender Identity and Urban Decay

Anjum's identity as a hijra places her at the intersection of multiple marginalities—gender, religion, and caste—and her occupation of the graveyard highlights the layered nature of social exclusion in urban India.

Cast out from her biological family and alienated within the hijra community after surviving the Gujarat pogrom, Anjum finds solace among the dead. Yet, rather than portraying this as tragic, Roy renders it an act of agency. "She had crossed over to the other side. The side that had only corpses for company" (Roy 28). In this metaphorical and literal crossing, Anjum does not succumb to erasure; she builds a life from what the city discards.

The graveyard itself becomes a symbol of urban decay—a reminder of the forgotten lives and histories buried beneath Delhi's glittering facade. But in Roy's narrative, decay is not death; it is compost for resistance. Anjum constructs a guesthouse within the graveyard, the Jannat Guest House, a name which ironically means "Paradise." This act is deeply political. By invoking paradise in a space of rot and ruin, Roy critiques the dystopia of urban neoliberalism, where development often means dislocation for the poor and the different. The guesthouse becomes a refuge for other outcasts—orphans, animals, the mentally ill—mirroring Anjum's own composite identity and reimagining kinship through shared marginality.

Intersections of Gender, Ecology, and Marginality

Roy's reconfiguration of the graveyard into a sanctuary for Anjum and others is more than an allegory for gender inclusion; it is an ecocritical gesture that underscores how gendered and ecological marginalities intersect. The graveyard, polluted and neglected, is feminized and queered through its transformation. Its association with decay parallels the treatment of transgender bodies in dominant discourse—as abject, expendable, and beyond social utility. Yet, by inhabiting and nurturing this space, Anjum queers the ecological narrative, turning wasteland into a home, a space of affective and communal regeneration.

Roy writes, "The Jannat Guest House and Funeral Services was not just a home. It was a sharing. A solidarity. A stubbornly living memory" (Roy 137). The graveyard becomes a relational ecology, where the marginalized co-exist not only with each other but also with the non-human—goats, peacocks, and plants—all thriving in this so-called zone of death. This multispecies coexistence challenges the anthropocentric bias in environmental discourse and foregrounds an alternative model of urban ecological engagement.

Narrative Reclamation

Through *The Ministry of Utmost Happiness*, Roy engages in narrative reclamation—restoring dignity to places and people relegated to the margins. The graveyard becomes a metaphor for India's discarded populations, but also for the possibilities of life and resistance that persist in overlooked spaces. Rather than succumbing to the logic of disposability, Roy offers a narrative in which survival is an act of political defiance. The city's forgotten spaces, she suggests, are not empty—they are full of memory, possibility, and resistance.

By centering the narrative in the graveyard, Roy displaces the conventional urban center as the locus of modernity. Instead, she proposes a new geography of hope, one built from below, from the peripheries. The novel asserts that these geographies, marked by decay and disrepair, are also the crucibles of care and creativity. Roy's work thus exemplifies how literature can function as a counter-cartography—mapping out the emotional, ecological, and political terrains of the marginalized in ways that reorient how we think about space, identity, and survival.

Hansda Sowvendra Shekhar's *The Adivasi Will Not Dance*: Resistance in the Forest

Land and Cultural Identity

Hansda Sowvendra Shekhar's *The Adivasi Will Not Dance* presents a literary landscape where land is not merely a resource but the living foundation of Adivasi identity, spirituality, and memory. In these stories, the forested terrains of Jharkhand—often seen as peripheral or backward in national discourse—emerge as deeply significant, both ecologically and culturally. The connection between the Adivasi and their land is neither metaphorical nor abstract; it is existential. As one character notes, "The forest is not outside of us. We are the forest. We are the river. We are the hill" (Shekhar 82). This intimate identification reflects an indigenous ecological consciousness in which human and non-human worlds are intertwined.

Such a worldview is starkly opposed to the developmentalist ethos that sees forests and mineral-rich landscapes as commodities to be extracted and converted into capital. The land, for Adivasi characters, is sacred and ancestral—a site of rituals, livelihoods, and collective memory. In Shekhar's narratives, losing the land is not only an ecological loss but a cultural and spiritual death. The rupture caused by displacement does not merely relocate bodies; it dismembers communities, severs traditions, and disorients cosmologies rooted in place.

Environmental Exploitation and Cultural Erasure

A central theme across the collection is the violence of resource extraction and the ways in which environmental degradation parallels social erasure. In several stories, mining companies arrive under the banner of "development," promising jobs and prosperity. However, the reality is exploitation, environmental ruin, and cultural disintegration. In "The Adivasi Will Not Dance," the titular character Mangal Murmu, a Santhal artist, recounts how his village is slowly consumed by the extractive ambitions of corporations: "The land where we once grew paddy has now become a field for machines. The river has gone dry. They have taken everything. And now they want our songs" (Shekhar 175).

This line encapsulates the dual process of ecological and cultural commodification. Not only is the land mined and defiled, but the rich traditions of Adivasi music, dance, and storytelling are also appropriated for state propaganda and tourist spectacle. Mangal's refusal to perform for the President is not a mere act of protest—it is a declaration of dignity, a refusal to be complicit in the commodification of his people's suffering. "We are not here to dance to their tunes while they take away our homes," he says (Shekhar 177), rejecting the tokenistic celebration of tribal identity that coexists with the systemic destruction of tribal life.

The environmental degradation depicted in the stories—deforestation, river pollution, loss of biodiversity—operates as a slow violence (Nixon 2), disproportionately impacting those already pushed to the social and economic margins. In Shekhar's work, ecological collapse is inseparable from caste and class hierarchies. The Adivasi do not experience environmental degradation as a distant or eventual threat; they live its consequences daily, in the air they breathe, the water they drink, and the soil they can no longer till.

Voices of Refusal

The stories in *The Adivasi Will Not Dance* function as acts of literary resistance. By foregrounding Adivasi voices, Shekhar contests the dominant narratives that define development through industrialization and assimilation. His characters refuse to be passive victims or romanticized relics; they articulate complex emotions—anger, grief, irony—and challenge the forces that seek to erase them. As literary scholar G. N. Devy observes, "When the languages and stories of tribal communities are ignored, what is lost is not merely speech but entire ways of seeing and being in the world" (Devy 44). Shekhar's fiction restores this vision by presenting Adivasi ways of knowing, being, and resisting.

Importantly, the mode of resistance in these stories is not always overt or confrontational. Sometimes, it manifests in small, quiet acts of defiance—refusing to move, continuing traditional rituals, telling stories in one's own language. These acts reclaim agency and challenge the logic of invisibility that often governs state and corporate approaches to the tribal question in India.

The forest, in Shekhar's work, is not a backdrop but a living entity—a witness, a sanctuary, and a casualty. By portraying the forest and its people as interconnected, Shekhar aligns ecological consciousness with cultural survival. His stories resist both the erasure of indigenous ecologies and the appropriation of Adivasi identity. In doing so, they redefine resistance not just as political speech but as narrative presence: to tell these stories, in one's own voice, is itself an act of survival.

Intersecting Axes: Ecology, Caste, Gender, and Indigeneity
Interdisciplinary Connections

Environmental injustice in 21st-century India is not a singular phenomenon; it is deeply embedded in intersecting systems of caste, gender, and indigeneity. The lived experiences of marginalized communities reveal how ecological collapse disproportionately affects those already burdened by systemic oppression. Through literature, these interconnections come into sharp focus. Whether it is the graveyard refuge of a transgender Muslim woman in Arundhati Roy's *The Ministry of Utmost Happiness*, the forested homelands of Santhals under siege in Hansda Sowvendra Shekhar's *The Adivasi Will Not Dance*, or the sewage-filled bastis in the verses of Meena Kandasamy and Yogesh Maitreya, each narrative highlights how environmental degradation is not only ecological, but also social, cultural, and political.

Anjum's story in Roy's novel is a case in point. Her identity as a transgender woman situates her at the margins of society, and her choice to live in a graveyard—a space of abandonment—recasts a site of decay as one of care and coexistence. In her world, "the boundaries between the living and the dead, the human and the non-human, blur" (Roy 234), suggesting an alternative mode of being rooted in interdependence. This queer ecology challenges not only gender norms but also anthropocentric and heteronormative environmental narratives.

Similarly, Shekhar's portrayal of Adivasi communities underscores how indigeneity is inseparable from ecological belonging. The Santhals' spiritual and cultural identity is entangled with the land they inhabit. Their displacement through mining is not simply an economic loss but a form of epistemic and ontological violence. As one character notes, "We were not just evicted from our land. We were told we had no right to exist as we are" (Shekhar 91). This articulation of dispossession foregrounds how indigeneity intersects with ecological injustice, making visible the historical continuity between colonial extraction and contemporary developmentalism.

Towards a Counter-Narrative

In challenging hegemonic narratives of development, the selected texts construct counter-narratives that center survival, care, and interdependence rather than exploitation and displacement. In place of the dominant discourse that equates "progress" with infrastructural expansion, industrialization, and urbanization—often at the cost of human and ecological lives—these literary works reimagine sustainability from the margins.

For instance, Roy's graveyard is not an apocalyptic wasteland but a sanctuary that thrives on mutual aid among outcasts—animals, humans, ghosts, and trees alike. This vision undermines the developmentalist fetish for sanitized, securitized urban spaces and instead suggests an ecology rooted in vulnerability and inclusivity (Roy 247). Similarly, Shekhar's narratives refuse to romanticize tribal life but insist on its value and viability against the forces of extraction. His characters are not passive victims but articulate agents who "will not dance" to the rhythm of imposed progress (Shekhar 176).

By foregrounding the voices of those at the "edge," these texts compel a redefinition of ecological thought in the Indian context. Literature, in this framework, becomes a site of ethical engagement—a space where the dominant epistemologies of development and sustainability are interrogated and reimagined. These narratives articulate a radical ecological consciousness that insists on justice—not only for the environment but for the people who inhabit its margins.

Conclusion

The literary works examined in this chapter—*The Ministry of Utmost Happiness* by Arundhati Roy, *The Adivasi Will Not Dance* by Hansda Sowvendra Shekhar, collectively reveal that peripheral geographies in 21st-century India are not merely sites of exclusion but dynamic terrains of survival, defiance, and reimagination. These texts disrupt dominant developmentalist narratives that associate progress with urbanization, industrial expansion, and ecological sacrifice. Instead, they recast wastelands, slums, mined forests, and graveyards as vital spaces where the marginalized assert presence and reclaim agency.

Through Anjum's occupation of a graveyard in Roy's novel, a transgender protagonist reconfigures a space of abandonment into one of sanctuary and interdependence, offering a radical alternative to neoliberal urban visions (Roy 234). Similarly, Shekhar's Adivasi characters resist cultural erasure and ecological displacement by anchoring their identities in land, memory, and oral storytelling (Shekhar 91). In Dalit poetry, polluted peripheries—whether caste-segregated colonies or toxic waters—become sites of poetic assertion, with Kandasamy and Maitreya transforming suffering into lyrical acts of resistance (Kandasamy 24; Maitreya 67). Collectively, these texts offer a counter-archive that redefines survival not as passive endurance but as active resistance—both ecological and existential.

This study contributes to the expanding field of ecocriticism by centering marginalized voices often absent from mainstream environmental discourse. Unlike traditional Western ecocriticism, which often romanticizes untouched nature or laments its degradation from a distance, the works discussed here engage with "wounded landscapes" intimately inhabited by those most affected by ecological collapse. These texts foreground Rob Nixon's concept of "slow violence", emphasizing the long-term, structural nature of environmental harm inflicted on marginalized communities (Nixon 2). By locating ecological crisis at the intersection of caste, gender, and indigeneity, this chapter broadens the scope of environmental literary studies, urging an ecocriticism that is historically grounded and socially responsive.

Moreover, the chapter adds depth to postcolonial literary studies by revealing how the legacies of colonial resource extraction persist in the form of modern displacement, land dispossession, and cultural suppression. Whether through Roy's critique of the Indian state's militarized urbanism or Shekhar's exposé of corporate mining in tribal lands, these texts extend the critique of empire into the ecological register.

In the context of Indian literary discourse, this chapter underscores the transformative potential of literature as a site of narrative reclamation. The literary reclamation of graveyards, forests, and polluted colonies serves not only to contest spatial marginalization but to rewrite the meanings of these spaces, infusing them with memory, resistance, and relationality.

The critical lens developed in this chapter opens pathways for further interdisciplinary research on marginal ecologies—including those affected by climate change, water crises, urban displacement, and agrarian distress. Future scholarship might explore regional literatures in vernacular languages to examine how localized environmental narratives intersect with caste and class structures. Additionally, collaborations between environmental humanities and social sciences could deepen our understanding of how literature not only represents but also participates in ecological activism.

Another promising avenue is the study of digital and oral storytelling traditions among marginalized communities, which may not conform to print culture yet are vital repositories of ecological knowledge and resistance. As India faces intensifying climate crises, it becomes even more urgent to amplify voices from the peripheries—not only to understand how survival is being redefined, but also to reimagine the possibilities of collective futurity.

Ultimately, the convergence of ecology, literature, and marginality calls for a decolonized ecocriticism—one that does not universalize suffering but attends to its specificities, histories, and voices. The texts examined here remind us that the periphery is not silent—it echoes, resounds, and speaks back with poetic, political, and ecological force.

References:

Kandasamy, Meena. *Ms. Militancy*. Navayana, 2011.

Maitreya, Yogesh. *Ambedkar 2021*. Panther's Paw Publication, 2021.

Nixon, Rob. *Slow Violence and the Environmentalism of the Poor*. Harvard University Press, 2011.

Roy, Arundhati. *The Ministry of Utmost Happiness*. Penguin Books, 2017.

Shekhar, Hansda Sowvendra. *The Adivasi Will Not Dance: Stories*. Speaking Tiger Books, 2015.

CHAPTER TWENTY-ONE

Dr. B.R. Ambedkar as the Architect of Dalit Literary Awakening

Dr.K.Thayalamurthy,
Assistant Professor of English
Government Arts and Science College
Thiruvennainallur, Villupuram.

Abstract

This paper explores the profound impact of Dr. B.R. Ambedkar on the emergence and evolution of Dalit literary consciousness in India. As a visionary social reformer, legal scholar, and the principal architect of the Indian Constitution, Ambedkar not only fought against caste oppression in political and legal spheres but also ignited a cultural and intellectual revolution among the marginalized. His philosophy, writings, and activism laid the ideological foundation for the Dalit literary movement, which emerged as a powerful form of resistance and self-expression for the oppressed castes. Through a critical examination of Ambedkar's influence in the Dalit literature, this paper highlights how his legacy continues to shape literature and inspire new generations of writers.

Keywords:

Dr. B.R. Ambedkar, Dalit Literature, Dalit Consciousness, Caste System, Social Justice, Literary Resistance, Ambedkarite Ideology, Identity Politics, Marginalized Voices, Human Dignity, Vernacular Expression, Autobiographical Narratives, Dalit Aesthetics, Caste Discrimination, Cultural Assertion.

Dr. B.R. Ambedkar as the Architect of Dalit Literary Awakening

The Indian caste system has historically silenced the voices of the marginalized, especially those from the Dalit communities. Literature, which often reflects societal structures, remained primarily inaccessible to Dalits until the 20th century. Dr. Bhimrao Ramji Ambedkar, one of the most influential thinkers and social reformers in Indian history, was more than a political leader—he was a visionary who ignited a cultural and literary awakening among India's most oppressed communities. He also emerged as a transformative figure who challenged the caste system and encouraged the Dalits to articulate their experiences through literature. His tireless fight against caste discrimination and his bold articulation of equality and human dignity laid the groundwork for what is now recognized as Dalit literature—a body of writing that speaks from the lived experiences of the marginalized. This paper investigates how Ambedkar served as the intellectual and ideological catalyst for developing Dalit literary consciousness.

Ambedkar's writings and speeches are not only political manifestos but also deeply intellectual texts that critiqued the hierarchical foundations of Indian society. His academic pursuits and political activism have deeply intertwined with his philosophical stance against caste-based discrimination. His seminal works such as *Annihilation of Caste* (1936), *Who Were the Shudras?* (1946), and *The Untouchables* (1948) offer a radical critique of the Hindu social order and analyze the origins and mechanisms of caste oppression with academic rigor and emotional force. These texts also inspired Dalits to critically examine their history, identity, and social condition—and, importantly, write about them.

Ambedkar's emphasis on rationalism, social justice, and equality resonated deeply with Dalit writers who sought to narrate their lived experiences of oppression and resistance. By challenging the moral legitimacy of the caste system and advocating for education, self-respect, and rights, Ambedkar gave Dalits a new language of assertion. He encouraged the oppressed to reject internalized inferiority and to express their stories unapologetically. This led to the emergence of Dalit literature as a distinct genre—marked by raw realism, emotional intensity, and political urgency. According to Nimbalker, one of the contemporary Dalit writers opines:

"The immense potential of Ambedkar and his philosophy, was not restricted to himself or anyone particular individual. He handed over to them the flares of his philosophy for development. His thoughts contained a graph of the progress of the people at the grass roots of the society. For this Doctor Ambedkar's life it-self has become a revolution. This revolution had changed the consciousness of the dalits. That is why Ambedkar and his philosophy is the source of Dalit literature". **(Limbale 19).**

Prior to his participation in the Southborough Commission, the Simon Commission, and the Round Table Conferences, Dr. B.R. Ambedkar had already laid the ideological and institutional foundations for the awakening of Dalit consciousness through a range of interventions. His early publications—*Mook Nayak, Bahishkrit Bharat, Janata*, and *Samata*—played a crucial role in articulating a counter-narrative to dominant caste ideologies. Simultaneously, his socio-political initiatives such as the establishment of the *Bahishkrit Hitkarini Sabha*, his symbolic entry into the *Kalaram Temple*, and the public burning of the *Manusmriti* became landmark moments in the assertion of Dalit identity and rights. Collectively, Ambedkar's life, work, and intellectual legacy catalyzed the formation of the Dalit movement and inspired a distinct Dalit literary consciousness.

Ambedkar's scholarly accomplishments and emancipatory politics made him a revered figure in the Dalit imagination. His image as a source of pride, dignity, and intellectual empowerment has been consistently reflected in Dalit literature, where he is often portrayed not only as a historical leader but as a symbolic and heroic presence. In Narendra Jadhav's autobiographical novel *Outcaste*, for instance, Ambedkar is depicted as a transformative figure—a catalyst in the revolutionary awakening of Dalit subjectivity. Throughout the narrative, Jadhav frequently references Ambedkar's struggles for social justice, positioning him as a moral and political compass for the oppressed.

The recovery of Dalit history during the uprisings of the 1990s generated significant debate within Dalit movements, particularly concerning their participation in mainstream electoral politics. Ilaiah (1998) observes that through their engagement in agrarian labour, Dalitbahujans maintain a constant and intimate relationship with the land. Their deep knowledge of the land—its productivity, colour, and composition—is, he argues, a crucial factor in enhancing agricultural yield. This recovery of history—including intellectual, political, and literary dimensions—exerted considerable pressure on the media, prompting renewed attention to the Dalit question. As Arjun Dangle asserts, Dalit literature is not merely a form of artistic expression; it is intrinsically linked to a broader socio-political movement aimed at bringing about transformative change.

Inspired by the teachings of Dr. B.R. Ambedkar, Dalit literature emerged as a distinct and powerful literary genre in the post-independence period, gaining significant momentum during the 1960s and 1970s in Maharashtra. This literary movement was marked by the proliferation of autobiographies, poetry, and fiction that foregrounded the lived experiences of caste-based oppression and social marginalization. Even decades after Ambedkar's death, his intellectual legacy continues to profoundly influence Dalit writers across linguistic and regional boundaries.

Prominent authors such as Omprakash Valmiki, Bama, Sharan Kumar Limbale, Namdeo Dhasal, Baburao Bagul, and Daya Pawar have extended the Ambedkarite tradition into diverse literary forms and socio-political contexts. These writers have explicitly acknowledged Ambedkar's enduring impact on their literary and ideological consciousness. Their works portray the brutal realities of untouchability, poverty, and systemic exclusion, and many of these texts have gained international recognition and academic legitimacy, featuring in university syllabi and global discussions on human rights and social justice.

In recent decades, a new generation of Dalit writers has emerged—one temporally distant from Ambedkar's era, yet deeply connected to his vision. Writers such as Yashica Dutt (*Coming Out as Dalit*), Meena Kandasamy (*The Gypsy Goddess*, *When I Hit You*), and Gogu Shyamala (short stories in Telugu) exemplify this contemporary wave. Their works continue to embody Ambedkar's principles of resistance, agency, and empowerment, while also expanding the thematic scope to include critical intersections with gender, sexuality, and globalization.

Autobiographical narratives have emerged as a powerful mode of political assertion within Dalit literature. Unlike the autobiographies of celebrities or historical figures, Dalit autobiographies such as *Joothan* (1997) by Omprakash Valmiki and *Teraskrit* (2002) by Surajpal Chauhan serve a fundamentally different purpose. These texts are not merely personal recollections but acts of collective resistance and identity formation.

As Gail Omvedt (1995) observes, there exists a prevailing sensibility that conflates Indian tradition with Hinduism, framing it as the Aryan heritage of Indian civilization. Dalit autobiographies challenge this dominant cultural narrative. Their emphasis is not on individualism in the conventional sense, but rather on linking personal experience to the collective struggles of the Dalit community. In doing so, these narratives interrogate the very foundations of Indian cultural and social hierarchies.

Moreover, many Dalit autobiographers experienced social mobility through education and eventually became part of the urban middle class. However, through the act of writing their life stories, they reaffirm their solidarity with their community and contribute to a broader politics of memory, identity, and empowerment. These autobiographies thus function both as personal testimony and as a means of mobilizing collective consciousness against systemic oppression.

Dalit literature is fundamentally characterized by its critical engagement with the caste system and all forms of social discrimination. It serves as a powerful instrument of social and political commitment, aiming to dismantle entrenched hierarchies and challenge the socio-cultural status quo. Rather than seeking aesthetic pleasure or intellectual sophistication for its own sake, Dalit literature foregrounds the realities of exclusion, marginalization, and the persistent denial of dignity and equality to the Dalit community. As Baburao Bagul eloquently asserted, Dalit literature is not driven by vengeance or hatred. He writes:

"Dalit Sahitya is not a literature of vengeance. Dalit Sahitya is not a literature that spreads hatred. Dalit Sahitya first promotes man's greatness and man's freedom, and for that reason it is a historic necessity... Anguish, waiting, pronouncements of sorrow alone do not define Dalit Sahitya. We need literature heroically full of life to create a new society." (Bagul xxi–xxii).

This vision underscores Dalit literature's role as a historical necessity, aimed at reconstructing society based on justice, equality, and human dignity. Dalit writers overwhelmingly believe that the principal purpose of literature is not entertainment or philosophical abstraction but social change. Accordingly, Dalit writing is deeply rooted in realism rather than romanticism and is unified in its exposition of systemic exploitation and caste-based discrimination.

By its very nature, Dalit literature exists on the margins of the literary mainstream, precisely because it critiques and confronts that very mainstream. Dalit writers have been highly critical of mainstream Indian literature's silence or romanticization of caste-based realities. Even when upper-caste writers such as Mulkraj Anand, Sane Guruji, or Sivshankar Pillai addressed Dalit issues, their representations were often perceived as patronizing, aimed at assimilating Dalit identity into a homogenized national narrative rather than amplifying authentic voices of resistance. As a result, such works are generally not considered representative of Dalit consciousness or emancipatory politics.

Language is another area where Dalit literature diverges from mainstream norms. Dalit writers frequently employ colloquial expressions, regional dialects, and linguistic registers deemed inappropriate by upper-caste literary standards. This choice is both aesthetic and political, asserting the legitimacy of marginalized voices and experiences in the literary domain. In recent decades, Dalit writers have also begun to develop critical frameworks and theoretical tools rooted in Dalit epistemologies, offering alternative ways of reading and evaluating literature.

Dalit literature draws ideological inspiration from both Ambedkarite and Marxist traditions, though Ambedkar's influence remains foundational. The literature is marked by themes of protest, identity, resistance, and the assertion of human dignity. It stands in direct contrast to the idealized portrayals of rural life and traditional social structures found in mainstream Indian literature. Instead, Dalit writing presents a stark, unflinching portrayal of social injustice, demanding recognition, redress, and radical transformation.

The integration of autobiographical elements, vernacular language, and uncompromising realism renders Dalit literature both powerful and accessible, grounding it in lived experience while making it relatable to a broad audience. Shaped profoundly by the vision and ideological legacy of Dr. B.R. Ambedkar, Dalit literature has consistently articulated themes that remain central to contemporary Dalit writing. Among these, several stand out:

Intersectionality: Contemporary Dalit literature increasingly addresses the interlocking structures of oppression, examining caste concerning gender, class, and sexuality, thus offering a more nuanced understanding of marginalization.

Reclamation of Identity: A prominent thematic concern is the assertion of Dalit identity and pride, involving the rejection of historically imposed stereotypes and the construction of self-defined narratives.

Resistance through Narrative: Both personal memoirs and collective histories serve as tools for challenging dominant historical discourses, transforming literature into a form of activism.

Critique of Institutional Oppression: Dalit literature rigorously critiques the persistence of caste-based discrimination in key societal institutions, including education, employment, and political structures.

Ambedkar's iconic exhortation to "educate, agitate, and organize" reverberates throughout Dalit literary expression, reinforcing literature's role as a vehicle for social justice and collective empowerment. In this context, Dalit literature transcends the aesthetic, functioning as a sociopolitical intervention and a form of cultural resistance.

Dr. B.R. Ambedkar stands not merely as a political figure, but as a profound cultural and intellectual force whose legacy continues to shape the consciousness of Dalit communities across India. His iconic call to "educate, agitate, and organize" transcended the realm of political mobilization to inspire a dynamic and transformative literary tradition. By encouraging Dalits to reclaim their voices and articulate their lived realities, Ambedkar laid the ideological and moral groundwork for a literary movement rooted in resistance, dignity, and social justice. His enduring influence positions him as the foundational catalyst of Dalit literary consciousness—a figure whose vision continues to inform and energize contemporary Dalit writing in its ongoing challenge to caste oppression and its affirmation of human worth.

Works Cited

Ambedkar, B. R. *Annihilation of Caste*. 1936.

---. *Who Were the Shudras?* 1946.

---. *The Untouchables: Who Were They and Why They Became Untouchables?* 1948.

Bagul, Baburao. "Dalit Literature is not Literature of Vengeance." *Poisoned Bread: Translations from Modern Marathi Dalit Literature*, edited by Arjun Dangle, Orient Longman, 1992, pp. xxi–xxii.

Dangle, Arjun, editor. *Poisoned Bread: Translations from Modern Marathi Dalit Literature*. Orient BlackSwan, 2009.

Dhasal, Namdeo. *Golpitha*. 1972.

Dutt, Yashica. *Coming Out as Dalit*. Aleph Book Company, 2019.

Gogu, Shyamala. *Father May Be an Elephant and Mother Only a Small Basket, But...* Navayana, 2006.

Guru, Gopal. *Humiliation: Claims and Context*. Oxford University Press, 2009.

Limbale, Sharan Kumar. *Towards an Aesthetics of Dalit Literature: History, Controversies and Considerations*. Translated by Alok Mukherjee, Orient Longman, 2004.

Jadhav, Narendra. *Outcaste: A Memoir*. Translated by Narendra Jadhav, Viking Penguin, 2003.

Kamble, Baby. *The Prisons We Broke*. Orient Longman, 2008.

Kandasamy, Meena. *The Gypsy Goddess*. Harper Perennial, 2014.

---. *When I Hit You: Or, A Portrait of the Writer as a Young Wife*. Juggernaut Books, 2017.

Limbale, Sharan Kumar. *Towards an Aesthetics of Dalit Literature: History, Controversies, and Considerations*. Translated by Alok Mukherjee, Orient Longman, 2004.

Nandy, Ashis. "Ambedkar and the Dalit Future." *Seminar*, no. 471, 1999.

Pawar, Daya. *Baluta*. 1995.

Patteeti, Rajasekhar, editor. *Exploring Fourth World Literatures: Tribals, Adivasis, Dalits*. Prestige Books, 2011.

Teltumbde, Anand. *Republic of Caste: Thinking Equality in the Time of Neoliberal Hindutva*. Navayana, 2020.

Valmiki, Omprakash. *Joothan: A Dalit's Life*. Translated by Arun Prabha Mukherjee, Samya, 2003.

---. *Joothan: An Untouchable's Life*. Cambridge University Press, 2008.

CHAPTER TWENTY-TWO

Portrayal of Immigration in Indian Writing in English and literary Contribution of Parsi Writers – A Study

M.Chinnadurai
Assitant Professor of English
Arignar Anna Govt Arts College,
Villupuram, Tamilnadu, India.

Abstract :
The word Immigration refers to the process of shifting to a new or unknown country with the intention of staying and living. There might be an unaccountable reason behind the migration such as to escape from religious persecution or a violent conflict, to have employment

opportunities abroad and for acquiring higher education. But it is important to understand that no people in any country or a region want to immigrate wholeheartedly. There must be a pain behind the immigration or the lock of opportunities in their native land. Assimilating in a new

country is not an easy task as it involves leaving one's distinct custom, culture and tradition. The paper focuses on the immigration of Parsis in Indian soil and the contribution of Parsis in the national Freedom Movement and in Indian English Literature in particular.

Key Words: Immigration, assimilation, ethnic-heritage, culture and custom.

Portrayal of Immigration in Indian Writing in English and literary Contribution of Parsi Writers – A Study

Introduction :

It is because of the poverty, the people move from one place to another place temporarily or permanently.migration is the movement of the people and it is linked with global issues including economic growth, poverty and religious persecution. Mrs.Priyambda Singh in her research paper states that " such people might be physically away from their own mother land.

The impact and the influence of age, psyche, cultural heritage and political up and down on the author's mind is due to the fact". Assimilation is the process whereby an ethnic heritage is

absorbed in to a dominant culture of the society. In country like India it had been such a long journey for Parsis to take asylum in the Indian soil. Absorbing a new identity is a challenging task for an ethnic community like Parsis. India is a country of multiculturalism where one could see the people of different races, languages, religions, classes and genders. It is unthinkable understand how the ethnic Parsis would have absorbed in the dominating multicultural Indian

society. It is only the Parsis who are known for their magnanimity and are kind hearted. They were loyal to the country where they settled as Zoroastrian Parsin in the new land India.

It is important to understand the way Parsis settled in the dominating multicultural Indian society. The Parsis are the Zoroastrians. The term ' parsi' is not a religion or a community rather it is a name addressed by the Indians as they were from the Persian land, now Iran. The ancient Persians were the native of the Southeastern portion of the Iranian Plateau and it had a number of tribes such as the Pasargadae, Maraphii and Maspii. Other tribes also were there but they were only the dependent of one of these major tribes. The nomadic Persians created the Achaemenid Empire. They were called as Iranian arrived in what is today Iran around 1000 BC. It is modern day Iran which is among the oldest inhabited regions like Damascus, Aleppo, Byblos, Argos, Athens, Sidon, Plodiv and Varanasi in the world. The Persian Empire is one of the greatest empires of the world which is as great as the Roman Empire of the ancient world.

It is also known as the Achaemenid Empire. The reign of the ruler could be calculated approximately between 559 BCE and 331B.C.E. It encompassed modern-day Iran, Egypt,Turkey and some parts of Afghanistan and Pakistan. It was Cyrus II under his leadership, the Persian

Empire emerged and he conquered the Median Empire reigned by his grand- father. After conquering the land he was called the 'shah' or the 'king' of Persia. Emperor Cyrus was not ruler; rather he showed love and mercy toward the lands and kingdoms he conquered. He also practiced religious and cultural tolerance toward the people whom he conquered. Then there came Darius, the relative of Cyrus, who set up a system of provinces and governors. The public works were made in his reign. It was under the rule of Xerxes, the son of Darius, who lost his ancestors glorious reign to Alexander the Great in 334 B.C.E. It was because of Xerxes' irresponsible and unsuccessful campaign to invade Greece.

Zarathustra was a priest and he founded the first monotheistic religion of the world 'Zoroastrianism'. He was addressed as a prophet who was also called as a messenger of the god and His commandments. It is also believed that he was the first one to reveal the religion in the world. Consequently there came other priest-turned prophets like Him. It was Moses for the Jews, Gautama Buddha for Buddhists, Wardhaman Mahavira for the Jains, Jesus Christ for the Christians, Mohammad for the Muslims and Guru Nanak for the Sikhs. The birth of these prophets are the result of God's plan. Thus the birth of Zarathushtra is a divine plan of Ahura Mazda. Zarathushtra is a word derived from Avastan, a language of Indo-Iranian, which has two meanings ; 'Possessing a wise camel' and ' A golden Star'. The two great religious teachers of the Persian Land called Kings Jamshed and Faridun predicted the prophet's arrival to the Earth. No definite record is found about his birth. However it has been estimated between the year 2000 BCE and 6000 BCE.

The full name of the holy prophet is Zarathushtra Spitama. 'Whitest or Purest' is the meaning of the name Spitama, which is also the name of the ninth ancestor of the Prophet. Gayomard, a king of Peshdadian Dynasty, who preached the people of the dynasty to have faith in one God ' Mazda'. The system of this faith is also called 'Mazdayasni' system. This religious belief system was highly encouraged and practiced by the great rulers of the Peshdadian dynasty like Hoshang, Jamshed and Faridun. The people lived happily until the Kayanian Dynasty.

During this dynasty, the evil power of Daevayasnis was predominant. The cruelty made by Daevayasnis was unbearable for Mother Earth 'Geush Urvan'. She cried to the Almighty who after discussion with Bahman and Ardibahesht, Ahura Mazda sent Zarathushtra to the Earth. It was said in various books and articles that Zarathushtra had seen the vision of Ahura

Mazda in his thirties when he was in meditation for months and that made him to aid the poor and needy to come over their problems in life. The Supreme lord of the universe Ahura Mazda fulfilled the divine mission by sending Zarathushtra as His medium. He was a man of God-intoxicated who wrote Gathas, seventeen Avestan Hymns traditionally believed to have been composed, and these verses are arranged in five different modes. It is written in Avestan Language. The language was spoken during Iran's Sasanian Era (226-651CE). His followers called Him Zarathustra, possessor of yellow or old camels. It was also believed in the case of the prophet's birth that his birth made nature rejoiced and all natural elements like trees, flowers, rivers were overjoyed. At the same time His birth made the demons trembled and frightened. Fairies and archangels came there to adore the laughing newborn baby. Miraculous happened in His birth. Attempts were made to kill the child by both the evil spirits and the king Turanian of Durasrobo. Like every messenger of the God he was saved miraculously in all their attempts.

Zarathushtra wanted to know the miseries of life. He had a deep longing for justice: why was there death and suffering in the world?; what was the origin of evil? Zarathushtra left home when he was twenty and he wandered like a cloud from land to land. He led a righteous survival. Controlling all his senses, he roamed and was seen in the forests, caves and top of the mountains. Ten years of calm meditation he did all the time. Once he received enlightenment from the vision of the supreme lord of the universe Ahura Mazda in the mountain of Sabatam. He conversed with the Supreme God and received His wisdom. In direct conversation with God he also received seven revelations. At the age of thirty, he was the full pledged renowned messenger of God Ahura Mazda. He obeyed and preached the commands of God. His preaching was terribly affected by the Satan of zoroastrianism, Ahriman who wanted to kill the God's messenger. Fortunately he overcame all his miseries with his spiritual power. Then he became the master even to the demons. The several archangels, the divine messengers of the Lord conversed with the prophet. They are ; Vohumanah – archangel of good thought; Asha Vahishta- the archangel of righteousness, commanded to protect the sacred fire; Khehathra Vairya- the archangel of good loyalty, commended to take care of the metals; Spenta Armaith- the archangel of modesty, who is presiding the Lord of the Earth; Hauravatat- the archangel of health and Ameretat- the archangel of immortality who presides over the plants. Three times he attained the celestial vision of God and he had a perfect knowledge of the whole universe. The sacred book Zend Avesta is like the Bible and Gita of the Zorostrians. The scholar R.C. Zaehner writes : ' Zoroastrianism is the religion of free will par excellence'.

The Chandogya Upanished, a story of a father who teaches his son the 'ultimate truth of Hinduism', has the similar experiences of the Zoroaster. The similarities between these two teachings are more or less common in its universal messages. Zoroaster travelled to many countries like China, India and he was not welcomed and appreciated by the people of the world. No one attempted to convert the religion of Zoroastrianism. Maidhyoi-Madnha, the cousin of the prophet who first converted into the religion. The two chief demon- worshipers Kavis and Karpans acted against the prophet and poisoned the ears of the Sovereign of Iran, Vishtasp to kill the prophet as he was the sorcerer. Believing the false accusation of the priests, the king also sentenced the prophet to die of starvation. When he was in prison, the favorite black horse of the king fell ill. He sent a message to the king that he would cure the horse if the king agreed to the four conditions of the prisoner Zoroaster. The four conditions are fulfilled. The king and the queen were ready to accept the new religion and they were convinced of the supernatural power of the prophet and started to worship Zoroaster as the prophet of Iran. It was not an exception to the Iranian Kingdom when the ruler of the kingdom practiced a new religion, the people also obeyed and worshiped Zoroastrianism. The new faith and beliefs spread far and wide. Zoroaster was pious and compassionate. Zoroster's main ethical teachings are: 'love the righteous. Have compassion for the distressed'.

It is very clear that assimilating in the Persian land became a terribly difficult task for Zoroastrians. The Zoroastrianism faith prevailed over the Persian land until the 8th century. It was the period of Arabian conquest. Right from the mid-seventh century, Muslim Arabs began to conquer the North of central Asia and West across African lands. The conquests were initiated by Muhammad, an Islamic Prophet. The Muslim conquest of Persia is also known as the Arab conquest of Iran. The Sasanian Empire came to an end and it led to the eventual decline of the Zoroastrian religion. The invading Arab conquests forced the zoroastrians to convert as Muslims. The age old Zorostrians were not ready to accept the new religion. However the Zoroastrians were free to worship Ahura Mazda without any obstruction. But in the second half of the seventh and first half of the eighth century the 'Umayyad Caliphs' introduced a ban on non-muslims who were all surviving in the Persian land. Thus the Arab soldiers quashed the Iranian insurgencies. They burnt the Zorostrian scriptures and the Zoroastrian priests were executed. Thus Islamic became the dominant religion in Persian land by the late middle ages. The native Zoroastrians were fleeing persecution that led many Zoroastrians to leave Persia altogether. In their own land the native Zoroastrians were forced to make decisions where they faced a dilemma to make a choice. They had only two options: whether to adopt the new religion or ready to die. The Parsis were known for their intelligence so they took a proper decision. The orthodox Zoroastrians could leave from the captivated land and immediately they were in search of such a land where they could survive with a primary need. Thus a large number of Zoroastrians emigrated to nearby India. The shipwrecked migrants landed in Diu, Gujarat carrying nothing but a Zoroastrian faith in their heart and a holy flame from their Fire Temple that they had left behind. Thus was their entry into Indian soil. India is a country with a power of assimilation of all irrespective of the race, religion,creed ect. Referring to India's plurality Salman Rushdie remarks: *'The idea of Indiai s based on multiplicity. Plurality and tolerance.... There can be no one way- religious, cultural and linguistic- of being an Indian; let difference reign'* P-14

In India the Persian Zoroastrian are called Parsis. It is because of the land from where they arrived. They reached Sanjan, a town in Gujarat,located on the banks of Maroli River where they were welcomed by the local Hindu Ruler Jadi Rana. An interesting apocryphal story is being told on settlement of the Parsis in India: when the newly landed Zoroastrians approached Jadi Rana for an asylum, the king gesticulated a vessel full of milk to signify that his kingdom was already full and cannot provide a space for the refugees. In response to the King, One Zoroastrian priest came forward and added a pinch of sugar to the milk indicating that they would not make the vessel to overflow rather they would make the native citizens sweeter and it also suggested that migrants would assimilate with the locals like 'sugar in milk'. The symbolic gesture of the Parsi-priest showed that if the immigrants were given shelter, they would further bring prosperity to the land. This soft kind approach of the migrants made the king happily move and be permitted to have asylum and to practice their own Zoroastrianism. The king also understood the new religious beliefs and customs which were new to the Indian land and the king was very pleased with the refugees.

The king asked the priest to narrate their literal requirements. The priest replied that they desired freedom as they were persecuted, freedom to bring up young generations in their own cultures and traditions, and they needed agricultural land for their survival as they would make them self-sufficient. On the requisition of the Parsis, the king allowed them to settle in Hindu land and agreed to those demands by imposing five preconditions. The five stipulations were:

1. The immigrants should adopt the local language 'Gujarati': (The Parsis also adopted Gujarati language and for generations they also have forgotten their traditional mother dialects. The census reports witness Gujarati was the mother tongue of Parsi Indians.)
2. The women should adopt the local dress 'the Sari': (Still a woman of traditional Parsi family wear sari in the Gujarati fashion which draped over the right shoulder with one end tucked at the back and the other end falls in the front).
3. They should never use arms against the host land. (They handed over all their weapons and kept their promised words even now).
4. The immigrant refugees were asked to venerate the cow as it was worshiped with great respect by the Hindu religion. (In regard to this condition, the traditional Parsi-Zoroastrians in order to respect the religious faith never take beef as their meat. It also be noted that there are no religious taboos against eating beef).
5. The marriage ceremonies should be performed during night only. (it was important to note the stipulation imposed by the king who thought that their subjects would not be attracted by such a ceremony and hence the danger of conversion would be minimized . This condition also favors the immigrants as they really do not want any Parsis to be converted to another religion and the local Hindus also will not convert into Zoroastrianism. In the subcontinent, the Parsis still perform their marriages during night only in their Fire Temples where the non-Parsis are not allowed even today).

The Parsi-priest accepted the conditions and founded the settlement of Sanjan. The Parsis were very much grateful to the king and the king was emotionally moved by their sincere commitment and soon he was allowed to settle in his kingdom. Later they erected their first Fire Temple in India. Later that Fire was taken to Udvada in the year 1742, the most important of its kind on the Indian subcontinent.

The process of assimilation in alien land was thus absorbed in this way by the 'Dustoor' a Parsi priest. The words of the dustoor are strictly followed by the assimilated parsis. Even today one could see the characteristic adaptability of this minority community which leads them to thrive in a country of such diverse culture and religion. It was also the reason behind India to become a secular country. But the Parsi critic, Nilufer Bharucha views that the conditions like adopting and obeying the customs, languages, dresses but not intermarry with the local population and never proselytizing led to feelings of alienation within the community. She points out that, ' These unequal conditions provide the ambivalent feeling of simultaneous identification with and alienation from india can be traced back to this rather oppressive agreement' (Bharucha, RM:EETS 26)

Bahman Kaikobad Hamjiar Sanjana composed a sacred verse, Qissa –i-Sanjan, an epic poem of eight hundred and sixty four lines completed in the year 1599. The verse recorded the existing account of the early years of Zoroastrian refugees in India. The composition of the verse witnessed that it might have been written at least six centuries after the arrival of the immigrants. An English translation was also made by E.B.Eastwick in the year 1844 and published in the first volume titled as *Journal of the Bombay Branch of the Royal Asiatic Society*. The immigrant Parsis must have originated from the Khorsan Province. The word Khorasan is a Persian name which means 'where the sun arrives from'. The Khorassan was also called Traxiane during the Parthhian and Hellenistic period. It was a province in Northeastern Iran. The region includes the present Iran, Afghanistan, Tajikistan, Turkmenistan and Uzbekistan.

Until the 17th century, the Parsis were called Zarthoshti, 'Zoroastrian' or Behdin ' Of good nature or religion in India. Assimilating in countries like India was a difficult task in their earlier periods. However they were in need of safeguarding their religion and their culture. Parsis are open minded and they are also known for their discipline and their helping tendency. They worked hard in the new land they settled. They utilized the opportunities properly. They acted wisely whenever the situation demanded. The commercial treaty made between the Mughal Emperor and James I of England was a great opportunity for the farming community, Parsis. They utilized the job offers of the British East India Company. The company leased the seven islands in Bombay from Charles II of England. In the east coast of the island, the company found a deep harbor and the Britishers were in the urge for settling up their first port in the sub-continent. The Prsis were very royal to the British. While the Indian languages were a barrier to their business, it was the Parsis who picked up the foreign

Language English quickly. In India, the Parsis were the first to embrace English language education and they became the most westernized community. They also trusted the Parsis and in turn the Parsis occupied a number of important posts in connection with the British Government and public works.

The role played by the Parsis in the national freedom movement was deeply considerable. Dadabhai Naoroji was one of the founders of the Indian national Congress. He was popularly known as 'Grand old man of India 'and 'Unofficial Ambassador of India'. He was the first Indian elected to the British Parliament, the first Indian to sit on a Royal Commission. In 1893, as the first Asian to occupy a seat in the British Parliament Naoroji spoke: '*Whether I am a Hindu, a Mohammedan, a Parsi, a Christian, or of any other creed, I am above all an Indian. Our country is India and Our nationality is Indian*'. The speech inspired many Indians and made Indians take an active part in the Indian freedom struggle movement. S.H. Jhabwala, another important figure in the national freedom movement who was jailed in the Meerut conspiracy. Bhikaiji Rustom Cama was one of the female activists in the Indian independence movement. She was the first Parsi woman who unfurled the first vision of the flag of Indian independence on August 21, 1907 in an international Socialist Conference held at Stuttgart, Germany.

On par with the diaspora, unlike other community, Parsi community encountered multiple diaspoas.at first the Diaspora from Iran to Gujarat where the Persians acquired the new identity as Parsi-Zoroastrians and had to live under a Hindu Dispension; then they spent under the muslim rulers of India, under the Mughal Empire. After this, their next diaspora was spent in British Colonial rule. From India they migrated to Canada as a south Asian origin. Notable Indian writers have migrated to Canada; they are Rohinton Mistry, Uma Paramesswari, Michael Ondaatjee, Himani Banerjee, Yasmin Ladha, Surjeet Kalsey and others. In the rapidly changing world scene, there needs to be a writer to maintain the identity of the Parsi community. There are a number of Parsi writers in India: Bapsi Sisdwa, Rohinton Mistry,Boman Desai, Bejan Daruwalla, Ardashir Vakil, Dina Mehta, D.F.Karaka, Nergis Dalal and others. All these Parsi writers are conscious about their identity crisis and they write with this realization. The contributions of these writers to literature are a lot. Their writings have brought them immense fame and placed them high in the social structure. all the works of these novelists reflect the history of India and their Parsi

Community in different ways.

Dosabhai Framji Karaka, an early parsi novelist and he was a reputed journalist. He wrote novels in the 1840s and 1850s. In England he wrote the book ' The Parsis: Their History , Manners, Customs and Religion' in 1858. This book provides an in-depth insight into the followers of the little known Zoroastrain faith which originated in ancient Persia. The object of this work is to make the English Public acquainted with the history, belief and manners of the Parsees who though unimportant in point of numbers they have their commercial habits, formed an important link between the English in India and the native inhabitants.

Nergis Dalal, a Parsi writer, has been writing for over fifty years. She was the author of four novels. In 1967, she wrote 'Minari' as her first novel. Minari was a fictitious place, but the descriptions are based on Mt.Abu. Dalal's other novels are: The Sisters, The Girls From Overseas and Skin Deep. Her last Skin Deep is a novel of psychological study of non-identical twins with a Parsi background. They also explore how societal perceptions of beauty influence attitudes and how the 'beautiful' twin is favored.

Perin Barucha, an Indian Parsi writer. She wrote only one novel titled 'The Fire Worshipers' published in 1968. The novel stressed on the customs of the Parsi community. The novel also portrays the problems in inter-caste marriages and the contentious issues of inter-faith marriages. The novel describes the Parsi Ethnicity in a rapidly changing India and how the Parsi community is experiencing a decline in its populations, or rather becoming assimilated into the greater society of the country. The novel also highlights the concept of ethical purity through the character of Nariman, an idealist, who wants to marry outside his family. Pestonji, the father of Nariman opposed the idea of marrying a Non-Parsi lady Portia Roy. Rohinton Mistry's Family Matters also deals with the same problem. Bharucha's The Fire Worshipers provides an interesting snapshot of the Parsi class structure in Post Independence Bombay.

Dina Mehta, a prominent stay-at-home Parsi novelist not an expatriate. She was the author of several short stories, novels and plays. In the city of Mumbai the playgoers are admired immensely by her play titled 'Brides are not for Burning'. Mehta's novel 'And Some Take a Lover' centers on a proposed inter-caste marriage between a sophisticated girl Miss.Roshni Wadia and the simple guardian boy Sudhir. The novel's typical Parsi paradoxes, identity crisis, apprehensions and political debates are beautifully discussed.

Keki N.Daruwalla, one of the most remarkable writers in India. Though he belongs to the Parsi Community, he prefers to be remembered as an Indian Poet in English. He doesn't pay much attention to his Parsi community; rather he rarely figures some references on The Tower Of Silence and other similar Parsi symbols.

Bapsi Sidhwa, called herself as a Punjabi-Parsi. She is a Pakistani American novelist who lives in the United States. She was born in Karachi,then a part of the British colony of India and she was brought up in the city of Lahore, Pakistan. Her works are: *Their Language of Love, Jungle Wala Sahib, City of Sin and Splendour: Writings on Lahore. Water, Cracking India* originally published as *Ice Candy Man* and the *Cow Eaters*. Her works focus on the life in colonial rule , the history and background of Partition, experiences of the Parsi Community and the experience of immigrating from south Asia to the United States. Many of the events in her novel resemble real occurrences of her life.

Firdaus Kanga, an Indian born British writer, was born in 1960 in Mumbai. He was an active journalist. His ' Trying to Grow' is a semi-auto-biographical novel set in India. It is a novel about a young Brit growing up with brittle bones. The protagonist of the novel is a boy of four feet who never grows. He finds his way into the world of sexuality and adulthood. The novel does not allow gender or disability to embed a growing Brit's desire for sex and love. The novel is set in, and describes humorously, the Parsi Community in Bombay. Kanga was the author of a travel book Heaven On Wheels about his experiences in London where he met Stephen Hawking. He is also an author of Godmen.

It is clear that all these Parsi writers, whether they are expatriates or stay-at-home Parsi writers, are consciously engaged in an active exploration of marginality. Rohinton Mistry, one of the diasporic and mainstream Indian writers of the Third world. It is the need of the day to understand the pangs of the declining Parsi community who are being thrown out from the mainstream dominant culture of the society. This research has taken the Indian born Canadian Novelist Rohinton Mistry for the study. Rohinton Mistry was the middle son of Behram Mistry and Freny Jhaveri Mistry born on July 3, 1952 in Bombay. Cyrus Mistry, a playwright and short story writer, is Rohinton's younger brother. Mistry's father was in the field of advertising and his mother was a homemaker like any Parsi mother of his community. Mistry recalls his mother in an interview with Angela Lambert: '*She was happy in that role doing the miracle that ball mothers perform of making what was barely enough seem like abundance. We didn't have new clothes and shoes as often as we might have liked but were certainly better off than the population'.* Mistry's mother might have been the model for some of his female characters. Dilnavaz in Such a Long Journey resembles Mistry's mother who manages to maintain the family afloat against all kinds of struggles.

The characters Mistry pictures in his Tales From Firozsha Baag are people of his own community and their rituals and they are portrayed that the characters are bound to their Zoroastrian religion. On seeing the identity forming elements of Parsiness, Kulke comments: " the Zoroastrian faith, a shared history of flight from Iran and feruge in India, a colonial elite consciousness and feelings of unease in decolonized India". It is not an exaggeration, if anyone says that Mistry's Tales From Firozsha Baag electrified the literary scene in the year 1987. It has a common thread of Parsi tradition, social practices, nostalgic experiences, the issues of the one and the young and the dilemma arising out of the migration. The characters in the collection are the mouthpiece of Mistry. He has no intention to expose the flaws in the characters, rather he tries to portray the realistic characters, though with no extraordinary accomplishments. The characters have the capacity to touch the hearts of the reader that is the success of the writer which Mistry has won uncountable readers.

Conclusion :

The Parsis had emerged as the foremost people in India in enriching the host land India and Indian English Literature. On par with the diaspora, unlike other communities, Parsi Community encountered multiple diaspora. At the outset it was from Iran to Gujarat where the

Parsis acquired the new identity as Parsi Zoroastrians and had to live under a Hindu Dispension; then they spent time under the muslim rulers of India, Under the Mughal Empire. After this, their next diaspora spent in British colonial rule. From India they migrated to various parts of the World as a south asian origin.wherever they move as a guest or a host they are welcomed as an Indian Parsi. The role played by the Parsis in the Indian National Movement and the contribution made by the Parsi writers to Indian English Literature are immense and most considerable.

<u>Works Cited</u>

Rushdie Salman . " Imaginary Homeland." London Review of Books 4.18(1982): 18-19. Web.26 Nov.2013.

Battachatya, Rebecca. " Bombay as Reflected in the Novels of Shobha De, Salman Rushdie and Rohinton Mistry" Vol.5.Issu 2.2017 (RJELAL).

Patterkine, Mamta. "Researching Rohinton Mistry: A Perfect blend of Facts and Fiction".Notion Press, Chennai 2019.

Mistry, Rohinton . Interview conducted by Nermeen Shaikh of Asia Source , November 1, 2007.

Kulke, E : History of the Parsis: A Minority as Agent of Social Change. Vikas Publishing House, Delhi, 1978.

Bhautoo-Dewnarain Nandini: " *Rohinton Mistry: An Introduction* . New Delhi: Foundation Books,2007. Print.

Steinberg, Sybil; Review of Swimming Lessons and Other Stories From Firozsha Baag. Publishers Weekly,1998.

Sethi, Sonika; Rohinton Mistry's Fiction: A Postmodern Approach. Notion Press, Chennai 2018.

Singh, Priyambda. Themes of Immigration in the novels of Rohinton Mistry; The Criterion: An International Journal in English. ISSN 0976-8165.

CHAPTER TWENTY-THREE

The Caste of Gender: Locating the Brahmin Woman Within Subaltern Discourse

Dr. M. P. Shabitha

Assistant Professor of English

Government Arts and Science College, Kallakurichi.

Abstract

This paper examines the paradoxical position of middle-class Brahmin women writers within Indian literary discourse through a comparative analysis of Shashi Deshpande's English novels and C.S. Lakshmi's (Ambai's) Tamil short stories. This paper adopts subaltern theory as a critical framework to investigate how these writers present the complex intersection of gender oppression and caste privilege. This critical examination exhibits that, though both writers express and articulate feministic values, their writings lie within the limitations of Brahminical feminism in addressing intersectional oppression. It also explores how the feministic thoughts and experiences shared in their writings locate the brahmin woman within the subaltern discourse. This paper concludes and acknowledges that women's subordination exists across hierarchies of caste, class, religion and region.

Keywords: feminism, brahmin, limitations, **Subaltern Discourse**

The Caste of Gender: Locating the Brahmin Woman Within Subaltern Discourse

Introduction:

Contemporary Indian women's writing has increasingly recognized the necessity of examining literary texts through intersectional frameworks that acknowledge the complex interplay of gender, caste, class, and regional identity in shaping women's experiences. This paper examines the work of two prominent Indian women writers—Shashi Deshpande and C.S. Lakshmi (who writes under the pseudonym Ambai)—through the critical lens of subaltern theory to investigate how their Brahminical positioning both enables and constrains their feminist literary narratives.

While substantial studies exist on both Deshpande and Ambai individually, this paper addresses how their Brahminical backgrounds inform their representations of women's experiences remain limited. This comparative approach offers valuable insights into how caste privilege operates within feminist literary discourse, often invisibly shaping narrative perspectives even in texts explicitly concerned with gender oppression. As Kancha Ilaiah Shepherd argues, "The mainstream Indian feminist discourse operates within Brahminical parameters... ignoring the specific oppressions faced by Dalit, Adivasi, and other marginalized women" (72). In this line, this paper inspects how such "Brahminical parameters" manifest in the literary works of Deshpande and Ambai, exploring the tensions and limitations that arise when caste privilege remains unexamined within feminist critique.

Theoretical Framework: Subaltern Studies and Intersectional Feminist Critique

This analysis employs subaltern theory as articulated by scholars such as Gayatri Chakravorty Spivak, Ranajit Guha, and Partha Chatterjee, alongside intersectional feminist theory as developed by Kimberlé Crenshaw and adapted to the Indian context by scholars such as Sharmila Rege and Uma Chakravarti. Subaltern studies provides a framework for examining how power operates through representation, while intersectional feminism enables analysis of how multiple systems of oppression interact simultaneously in women's lives.

Spivak's seminal question—"Can the subaltern speak?"—and her critique of intellectuals who presume to represent subaltern subjects proves particularly relevant when examining authors whose social positioning grants them certain privileges even as they experience gender discrimination (271-313). Similarly, Chakravarti's concept of "Brahminical patriarchy" offers a framework for understanding how gender and caste hierarchies mutually reinforce each other, creating distinct forms of oppression that cannot be addressed through gender analysis alone (27-38).

The Double-Edged Sword of Brahminical Feminism

Both Deshpande and Ambai write primarily about middle-class Brahmin women, inadvertently reinforcing Brahminical cultural markers through their characterization, naming practices, and narrative focus. As Spivak notes, the relationship between vernacular and Indo-Anglian literature represents a "site of class-cultural struggle" in the production of cultural identity (qtd. in Mukherjee 200). This struggle is evident in how both authors simultaneously critique and reinforce Brahminical social structures.

The protagonists in Deshpande's *That Long Silence* (1989) and *The Dark Holds No Terrors* (1990) embody this tension. Characters like Jaya and Sarita experience the silencing effects of patriarchy while simultaneously benefiting from their caste position. Similarly, Ambai's stories like "A Kitchen in the Corner of the House" feature Brahmin women like Minakshi who challenge patriarchal norms while remaining insulated from broader caste oppression.

Textual analysis reveals how Brahminical markers permeate both authors' work. Deshpande's novels feature explicitly Brahmin characters with names such as Jaya, Vanitamami, Sarita, and Madhav. Her narratives frequently reference Brahminical customs and rituals, as when Sarita recalls being isolated during menstruation—a practice with explicit caste dimensions. Similarly, Ambai's stories are populated with characters named Chidambaram, Krishnamoorthy, and Minakshi, and frequently reference Brahminical spatial arrangements, particularly kitchen spaces that are central to maintaining caste purity.

Following Spivak's concept of the "subaltern woman," we can observe how Brahmin women occupy a liminal space—subordinated within their caste structure yet positioned above lower-caste women in the social hierarchy. This creates what Crenshaw would identify as an intersectional blind spot, where caste privilege obscures a comprehensive understanding of women's oppression across different social strata.

Gendered Subalterns: The Paradox of Privileged Marginality

Applying Ranajit Guha's framework of subalternity, Brahmin women as depicted by Deshpande and Ambai constitute what might be termed "privileged subalterns"—subjects who experience gender-based marginalization despite their caste advantage. This paradox is evident in Deshpande's portrayal of Sarita in *The Dark Holds No Terrors*, who reflects: "Not just because of paraiyah, with my special cup and plate by my side in which was served from a distance for my touch was, it seemed pollution" (62).

Here, Sarita's menstruation relegates her temporarily to the status of a Dalit ("paraiyah"), revealing how patriarchal Brahminism creates internal hierarchies even within privileged castes. This moment inadvertently exposes the convergence of caste and gender oppression—the same logic of purity and pollution that excludes Dalits operates within Brahmin households to control women's bodies. However, unlike true subalterns in Spivak's formulation, these characters possess educational capital and cultural authority that provides avenues for resistance unavailable to lower-caste women.

Ambai's characters similarly exhibit this tension. In "Once Again," she criticizes gender construction through the characters of Lokus and Sabari, yet her critique remains primarily focused on gender without substantively addressing how caste compounds women's oppression. As Antonio Gramsci might observe, this represents a form of "contradictory consciousness" where progressive gender politics coexist with unexamined caste privilege (Gramsci 326-27).

This analysis reveals how both authors inhabit what Bourdieu would term a "dominated fraction of the dominant class" (Distinction 372)—subordinated by gender while simultaneously benefiting from caste capital that facilitates their literary careers and shapes their narrative perspectives.

Beyond the Family: Divergent Approaches to Feminist Resistance

A significant difference between Deshpande and Ambai lies in their respective approaches to feminist resistance. Deshpande's characters primarily navigate oppression within domestic spaces, seeking liberation through psychological self-realization rather than structural change. Her protagonists like Jaya and Sarita ultimately return to their marriages after periods of critical reflection, suggesting reform rather than revolution.

The resolution of *That Long Silence* exemplifies this approach. After a period of introspection triggered by her husband's professional disgrace, Jaya ultimately decides to break her silence and assert herself within her marriage rather than abandon it. As she reflects: "We don't change overnight. It's possible that we may not change even over long periods of time. But we can always hope. Without that, life would be impossible" (Deshpande, *That Long Silence* 193). This individualistic approach to resistance emphasizes psychological transformation over collective political action.

Conversely, Ambai's characters more frequently confront systemic oppression beyond the family unit. In stories like "Black Horse Square" and "Age," she portrays women engaged in political resistance against state violence. The Marathi activist Rosa in "Black Horse Square" rejects legal remedies after police torture, declaring: "To whom are you asking me to plead for justice? To those whom destroyed me?... I am not the one who pleads permission, I grab it" (Ambai 138).

This distinction reflects what Partha Chatterjee identifies as the differentiation between the "ghar" (home) and "bahir" (world) in nationalist discourse (238-39). While Deshpande's feminism operates primarily within the "ghar," Ambai more frequently ventures into the "bahir" of political resistance. However, neither fully addresses how caste shapes these experiences differently for non-Brahmin women.

As Sharmila Rege notes, "The experiences and struggles of Dalit women against the interconnected oppressions of caste, class and patriarchy remain invisible or marginal to mainstream feminist theory and politics" (44). This invisibility is reproduced in both authors' works, albeit in different ways.

Language, Readership, and Subaltern Representation

The linguistic choices of these authors create different relationships to subaltern representation. Deshpande, writing in English, reaches a broader international audience but potentially alienates herself from lower-class Indian readers. Ambai, writing in Tamil, maintains a connection to regional linguistic communities but faces limitations in global reach.

This linguistic divide exemplifies what Aijaz Ahmad identifies as the "three-worlds theory" problem in postcolonial literature—where writing in English positions authors within global capitalist literary markets while potentially disconnecting them from local concerns (In Theory 93-94). As Ambai herself acknowledges: "Sometimes Tamil writers feel that they are promoted to next level when their works get translated into English" ("Challenging the Stereotyped Women").

The question of readership becomes central to understanding these authors' relationship to subalternity. Deshpande's English-language novels enjoy wider international circulation, giving her greater visibility but potentially making her work less accessible to the very subaltern subjects she sometimes represents. Ambai, working in Tamil, maintains a connection to regional readers but struggles for wider recognition.

This dichotomy reflects what Pascale Casanova terms the "world republic of letters"—a transnational literary field structured by unequal power relations between languages, where English occupies a hegemonic position (The World Republic of Letters 4-5). Within this hierarchical system, Indian English writing often receives greater critical recognition than regional language literature, regardless of content or quality.

Modernism, Tradition, and the Search for Authentic Voice

Both writers employ modernist techniques like stream of consciousness and fragmented narratives while addressing traditionally silenced aspects of women's experience. However, their relationship to modernism reveals different approaches to subalternity.

Deshpande's modernism operates within a relatively conventional narrative framework that privileges psychological realism over formal experimentation. Her characters like Jaya and Sarita engage in extended interior monologues that reveal their psychological struggles, but the novels ultimately reaffirm traditional family structures. As Jasbir Jain observes, "Deshpande's novels operate at the interstices of tradition and modernity, neither fully embracing nor completely rejecting either paradigm" (117).

Ambai's modernism extends to both form and content. In stories like "Vamanan," she integrates scientific themes with feminist critique, challenging gender binaries at both ideological and formal levels. Her experimental approach to narrative voice in "Once Again" creates what Homi Bhabha might call a "third space" that disrupts binary gender constructions (Bhabha 37).

As Ambai writes in "Once Again": "In that cold late evening thickly spread with stars, a birth took place, true to its time" (125). This "birth" represents the potential for new subjectivities beyond the binary gender constructions imposed by dominant discourse—what Spivak might call a "strategic essentialism" that acknowledges constructed identities while working toward their dissolution ("Subaltern Studies" 13).

Silence, Voice, and the Limits of Representation

The theme of silence pervades both authors' works, reflecting what Spivak identifies as the fundamental problem of subaltern representation—"the subaltern cannot speak" (308). Deshpande's title *That Long Silence* directly addresses the enforced muteness of women within patriarchal structures. Her protagonist Jaya reflects: "My relationship with this man...refused to take any shape at all: it just slipped about, frighteningly fluid" (Deshpande, *That Long Silence* 151).

This fluidity represents both the potential for liberation and the difficulty of articulating female experience within patriarchal language. As Michel Foucault might observe, Jaya's struggle is not merely for the right to speak but for access to discursive structures that would make her speech meaningful (Power/Knowledge 82-83).

Ambai's approach to silence is more explicitly political. Her characters in "Black Horse Square" and "Age" confront silencing through state violence and torture. When the activist Rosa refuses to file a police complaint about her torture, she rejects not only legal remedies but the discursive framework that positions her as a victim rather than an agent.

Both authors thus engage with what Spivak terms the "epistemic violence" of representation—the impossibility of authentically representing subaltern experience without reinforcing the very power structures that create subalternity ("Can the Subaltern Speak?" 280-81). Their different approaches reflect varying responses to this fundamental problem.

Conclusion

This comparative analysis reveals how both Deshpande and Ambai navigate the complex terrain of gender, caste, and linguistic privilege in their representation of women's experiences. Their works demonstrate the limitations of Brahminical feminism in addressing intersectional oppression while simultaneously offering valuable insights into the psychological and social dimensions of gender subjugation.

To transcend these limitations would require what bell hooks terms a "margin to center" approach—one that centers the experiences of those who face multiple forms of oppression rather than privileging single-axis analyses of gender (15-22). Such an approach would recognize how caste, class, religion, and regional identity intersect with gender to create complex conditions of oppression and resistance.

Works Cited

Ahmad, Aijaz. *In Theory: Classes, Nations, Literatures*. Verso, 1992.

Ambai. *The Purple Sea: Short Stories by Ambai*. Translated by Lakshmi Holmstrom, Affiliated East-West Press, 1992.

Bhabha, Homi. *The Location of Culture*. Routledge, 1994.

Bourdieu, Pierre. *Distinction: A Social Critique of the Judgement of Taste*. Translated by Richard Nice, Harvard University Press, 1984.

Casanova, Pascale. *The World Republic of Letters*. Translated by M. B. DeBevoise, Harvard University Press, 2004.

Chakravarti, Uma. "Conceptualising Brahmanical Patriarchy in Early India: Gender, Caste, Class and State." *Economic and Political Weekly*, vol. 28, no. 14, 1993, pp. 27-38.

"Challenging the Stereotyped Women." *The Hindu*, 2005.

Chatterjee, Partha. "The Nationalist Resolution of the Women's Question." *Recasting Women: Essays in Indian Colonial History*, edited by Kumkum Sangari and Sudesh Vaid, Rutgers University Press, 1990, pp. 233-253.

Crenshaw, Kimberlé. "Mapping the Margins: Intersectionality, Identity Politics, and Violence Against Women of Color." *Stanford Law Review*, vol. 43, no. 6, 1991, pp. 1241-1299.

Deshpande, Shashi. *That Long Silence*. Penguin Books, 1989.

---. *The Dark Holds No Terrors*. Penguin Books, 1990.

Foucault, Michel. *Power/Knowledge: Selected Interviews and Other Writings 1972-1977*. Edited by Colin Gordon, Pantheon Books, 1980.

Gramsci, Antonio. *Selections from the Prison Notebooks*. Edited and translated by Quintin Hoare and Geoffrey Nowell Smith, International Publishers, 1971.

Guha, Ranajit. *Elementary Aspects of Peasant Insurgency in Colonial India*. Oxford University Press, 1983.

hooks, bell. *Feminist Theory: From Margin to Center*. South End Press, 1984.

Ilaiah Shepherd, Kancha. *Why I Am Not a Hindu: A Sudra Critique of Hindutva Philosophy, Culture and Political Economy*. 2nd ed., Sage Publications, 2019.

Jain, Jasbir. *Writing Women Across Cultures*. Rawat Publications, 2002.

Mukherjee, Arun. "The Exclusions of Postcolonial Theory and Mulk Raj Anand's 'Untouchable': A Case Study." *ARIEL: A Review of International English Literature*, vol. 22, no. 3, 1991, pp. 27-48.

Rege, Sharmila. *Writing Caste/Writing Gender: Narrating Dalit Women's Testimonios*. Zubaan, 2006.

Spivak, Gayatri Chakravorty. "Can the Subaltern Speak?" *Marxism and the Interpretation of Culture*, edited by Cary Nelson and Lawrence Grossberg, University of Illinois Press, 1988, pp. 271-313.

---. "Subaltern Studies: Deconstructing Historiography." *Selected Subaltern Studies*, edited by Ranajit Guha and Gayatri Chakravorty Spivak,

Oxford University Press, 1988, pp. 3-32.

Subalternity and Urban Margins in Kunal Basu's Kalkatta

A Stanley Edward Rayen,
Lecturer in English,
Dept of Basic Engineering,
Govt Polytechnic College, Kooduveli, Cuddalore.

Abstract

This research paper examines Kunal Basu's *Kalkatta* (2015) through the lens of Subaltern Studies and intersectionality, focusing on marginalized identities shaped by religion, gender, class, and statelessness in postcolonial urban India. Centralizing the life of Jamshed "Jami" Alam, a Muslim refugee and undocumented immigrant, the study reveals how systemic exclusion, socio-political dislocation, and identity formation intersect in contemporary Kolkata. It also explores the role of Rani, a transgender character, in portraying gendered subalternity. By analyzing key passages and employing the theories of Gayatri Chakravorty Spivak, Ranajit Guha, and Kimberlé Crenshaw, the paper argues that the novel amplifies subaltern voices while questioning the structures that silence them. The unconventional spelling in the title—*Kalkatta*—signifies an alternative geography of the city viewed from its margins.

Keywords: Subaltern Studies, intersectionality, undocumented migration, transgender identity, urban marginality, postcolonial literature, Kolkata.

Subalternity and Urban Margins in Kunal Basu's Kalkatta

Introduction

Kunal Basu's *Kalkatta* offers an unflinching portrayal of Kolkata's underrepresented communities: Muslim refugees, undocumented immigrants, hijra individuals, and the urban poor. Departing from romanticized visions of the city, Basu's narrative foregrounds dislocation and identity struggles. In the spirit of Gayatri Chakravorty Spivak's provocative inquiry—"Can the Subaltern Speak?"—the novel ventures into giving voice to those who are historically silenced. Through the first-person perspective of Jami, an undocumented Bangladeshi immigrant, Basu crafts a rare insider account of socio-economic marginality.

Theoretical Framework: Subalternity and Intersectionality

Subaltern Studies, as developed by Ranajit Guha, seeks to document the lives of those excluded from elite historiographies. Spivak's critique deepens this framework by emphasizing epistemic violence and the compounded marginalization of gendered subalterns. She asserts that "the subaltern as female is even more deeply in shadow," cautioning that representation risks erasure if not handled critically. Kimberlé Crenshaw's concept of intersectionality enhances this inquiry by illustrating how overlapping identities—religious, sexual, class-based—construct unique modes of oppression. In *Kalkatta*, both Jami and Rani represent such intersectional identities.

Muslim Refugees and Generational Displacement

Jami's refugee lineage—traced from Bihar to East Pakistan and finally to Dhaka's Geneva Camp—exemplifies inherited statelessness. His mother's yearning for citizenship is encapsulated in her words: "Our Jami can become prime minister of Kalkatta, whereas here he'll only be a bus driver if he's lucky." Their illegal migration to Kolkata results in forged documents, making Jami's existence both possible and precarious. His father ominously tells him, "Your birth certificate could become your death certificate." This underscores how bureaucracy serves as a tool of inclusion and exclusion for subaltern groups.

Kalkatta as a Divided Urban Space

The spelling "Kalkatta" signals the city as experienced by non-elite inhabitants. Jami's neighborhood, Zakaria Street, is depicted as "a ghetto within the city, vibrant but invisible." The novel contrasts this world with elite spaces like Alipore, demonstrating Kolkata's fractured geography. At school, Jami is told that Bengali Hindu boys "won't like you sitting beside them," exposing the intersection of ethnic and religious bias. His efforts to fit in—learning Bengali, changing his accent, hiding his origin—show the cost of assimilation.

Gendered Subalternity: Rani and the Hijra Narrative

Rani, a transgender woman and Jami's confidante, introduces readers to the hijra community's struggles. She recalls: "People like me are neither men nor women. We are shadows." Her mother's refusal to send her to a hijra commune spared her from exploitation, but not from systemic exclusion. Rani becomes Jami's emotional anchor, offering care and wisdom. Their relationship exemplifies solidarity across marginalized identities and reflects what Spivak calls the "conditions of impossibility" under which subalterns may still find voice and connection.

Intersectionality in Marginal Lives

Jami's marginality is multilayered: Muslim, undocumented, working-class, and employed in the sex industry. Rani faces compounded oppression as a poor transgender woman. Yet within this space of vulnerability, the two form a chosen kinship. "Rani was the only one who saw me whole," Jami reflects, acknowledging how intersectional experience can also generate empathy and resilience. Their bond signifies a form of resistance—affective, ethical, and political.

Title Justification: "Kalkatta" as Subaltern Mapping

The title *Kalkatta* is not a misspelling but a political statement. It reflects how the city is pronounced by its working-class and migrant residents, reclaiming linguistic space from colonial (*Calcutta*) and elite nationalist (*Kolkata*) narratives. Jami's journey across the city's literal and metaphorical boundaries—the ghettos, massage parlors, elite drawing rooms—charts an alternative urban cartography shaped by exclusion, aspiration, and negotiation.

Conclusion

Kalkatta reimagines the urban novel through the lens of subalternity. By foregrounding undocumented migrants, religious minorities, and transgender individuals, Kunal Basu offers a complex narrative that resists simplistic categorization. Jami and Rani's stories reveal the fragility of belonging in a city that appears inclusive but functions through stratification. While Spivak warns of the difficulty of truly hearing the subaltern, *Kalkatta* demonstrates that fiction can carve out spaces where such voices resonate. The novel's title, tone, and structure collectively map the city from its margins, offering both critique and testament

Works Cited

Basu, Kunal. *Kalkatta*. Picador India, 2015.

Crenshaw, Kimberlé. "Mapping the Margins: Intersectionality, Identity Politics, and Violence Against Women of Color." *Stanford Law Review*, vol. 43, no. 6, July 1991, pp. 1241–1299. JSTOR, https://doi.org/10.2307/1229039.

Guha, Ranajit. "On Some Aspects of the Historiography of Colonial India." *Subaltern Studies I*, edited by Ranajit Guha, Oxford UP, 1982, pp. 1–8.

Spivak, Gayatri Chakravorty. "Can the Subaltern Speak?" *Marxism and the Interpretation of Culture*, edited by Cary Nelson and Lawrence Grossberg, U of Illinois P, 1988, pp. 271–313.

The Unseen Scars: Investigating the Struggles of the Underprivileged in Rohinton Mistry's A Fine Balance

Mr. S. Ranjithkumar[1],
Guest Lecturer in English,
Government Arts and Science College,
Thiruvennainallur, Villupuram.
Mr. S. VIJAYA SARATHI[2],
Guest Lecturer in English,
Government Arts and Science College,
Thiruvennainallur, Villupuram.

Abstract

This paper offers a critical examination of the struggles faced by marginalized communities within the context of Hinduism, particularly focusing on the oppression of Dalits. It aims to reveal the cruel and unjust treatment these individuals endure under caste supremacy. Using Rohinton Mistry's novel *A Fine Balance* as a lens, the paper highlights the systemic abuse, discrimination, and dehumanization faced by Dalits in India, shedding light on both social and economic injustices.

Keywords: oppression, poverty, caste-prejudice, dominance, helplessness

The Unseen Scars: Investigating the Struggles of the Underprivileged in Rohinton Mistry's A Fine Balance

In *A Fine Balance*, Rohinton Mistry crafts a narrative that lays bare the dehumanizing impact of the caste system and authoritarian politics on the most vulnerable members of society. The novel, set during India's Emergency in the mid-1970s, becomes a stark commentary on the deep divide between privilege and poverty. Through characters like Ishvar, Omprakash, and Dukhi Mochi, Mistry offers a visceral portrayal of generational trauma, caste violence, and lost hope. It is also a deeply moving novel that combines four key characters—Dina Dalal, Ishvar, Omprakash, and Maneck Kohlah—from various social and caste backgrounds. Their shared experiences of trauma, loss, and hardship draw them together in Dina's apartment, hoping for stability and a better future. However, the imposition of Emergency disrupts their fragile lives, leading to devastating consequences. Each character undergoes severe emotional and physical suffering due to societal and political turmoil.

Untouchability, rooted in the caste system, subjects an entire community to exclusion and humiliation. Higher-caste individuals believe even the presence or touch of a lower-caste person can defile them. Dalits are barred from public spaces, including streets, temples, and even communal wells, facing abuse and punishment for simply existing. Among the most tragic figures are Ishvar and Omprakash, members of the Chamaar caste—traditionally cobblers and seen as "untouchables." Their work revolves around processing dead animals, which further entrenches their social stigma. Their lives are defined by poverty, discrimination, and trauma.

Mistry delves into the cruelty of caste hierarchies through the story of Ishvar and Omprakash, descendants of Chamaar cobblers. Their journey from a rural village to a bustling city is marked by exploitation, humiliation, and systemic rejection. Despite their skills and aspirations, they are constantly reminded of their place in a rigid social order, such as "They had learned to be invisible, to avoid being seen, for being seen could mean being punished, simply for existing" (146). This powerful line encapsulates the inner world of the oppressed—those who must navigate daily life with fear, shame, and invisibility.

Dukhi Mochi, Ishvar's father, is all too aware of the caste-based violence and suffering. His wife, Roopa, is forced to steal food to feed her children and is brutally raped by a landlord's watchman. This act of sexual violence is shown as a twisted form of caste-based punishment, revealing the hypocrisy of those who deem Dalits impure but exploit them in the most intimate and violent ways. Mistry condemns this cruelty through the character of Roopa, whose assault exemplifies the gross injustice inflicted upon lower-caste women. Her pain, and Dukhi's helplessness, underscores the silent suffering of many such families. Roopa's assault, highlighting both gendered and caste-based oppression:

They called her a thief, and when she pleaded for mercy, the watchman dragged her behind the haystack and raped her. He said that was the punishment for Chamaar women who dared to trespass. (AFB P.147)

This is significant because it reflects the intersection of caste and gender, where Dalit women face not only social exclusion but also become targets of sexual violence as a form of punishment and control. Mistry uses such moments to expose the hypocrisy and cruelty within the caste hierarchy—those deemed "untouchable" are paradoxically exploited in the most intimate and violent ways.

Sexual oppression and the evils of Casteism, particularly the Brahmanical dominance in the society are two main aspects in this part of the novel. The lower caste women had to go to the upper caste without any protest. Protests faced severe torture also. Lower-caste women had no self-respect in the eyes of the upper class. In the village one could often hear such types of talking, "She refused to go to the field with the zamindar's son, so they shaved her head and walked her naked through the square". (AFB P.96) Roopa, Dukhi's wife faced sexual torture while stealing milk for his newborn babies at night. Roopa had to steal milk from the upper-class house for her infants, otherwise, they would starve. She had to pay for that. One day she was caught red-handed by the guard and fearing the torture of the upper class she paid herself to the gardener as punishment.

Casteism among the lower castes is another important aspect of the paper. It is an important thing for analysis. Very often it is seen that there is a competition or superiority felt by the lower castes among themselves in the society. Categorisation among the lower castes is seen in the novel Untouchable by Mulk Raj Anand. Here Anand portrays the character of Bakha who clears the drains in the society and shows how he is humiliated by the other lower castes there. The same thing is to be seen in this part of the novel. Roopa disagreed that his son Narayan would seek the caste Bhunia as they were regarded as lower to them.   But this Caste prejudice did not work for Roopa and she was corrected by her son. "I think I should sew for anybody who comes to me, Brahmin or Bhunghi." (AFB P.133) The others reminded Roopa that it was the same thing that they had to tolerate from the upper-class takers. So, they must not possess such a kind of prejudice in their minds. Momentary happiness the great novelist Thomas Hardy believed that happiness is a momentary and transient part of life.

Two leather-workers turned tailors, Ishvar and Omprakash are the victim of their circumstances. Story starts with Dukhi Mochi who lives under terror and suppression. He is unable to hear more humiliation; he goes to Pandit Lalluram for seeking justice. Pandit tells him that one should do according to the dharma/religion. That's why he sends his son Narayan to Ashraf in the nearby town so that they may become tailors and get rid of their family profession of leather work. After becoming a tailor Narayan returns to the village and opens his shop for sewing the clothes. He does not sew the clothes for the upper caste people. He finds many changes in the village but his father says that nothing has changed for the poor Dalit people:

Your life, my life. Your occupation, from leather to cloth... More than twenty years have passed since independence. How much longer? I want to be able to drink from the village well, worship in the temple, walk where I like ... Son; those are dangerous things to want. You changed from Chamaar to tailor. Be satisfied with that. Narayan shook his head. That was your victory (174-175).

Narayan takes a very bold step in the village. He declares his own independence in the village. He does not want to vote for the upper caste people. He wants to vote for the candidate of his choice but this mistake by him proves very dangerous to him. Thakur Dharmdasi gets angry with him and his goons took him and two of his companions to Thakur's flat. They are tied with a rope upside down on a banyan tree. They are made without clothes and are badly beaten throughout the day and when Thakur Dharmdasi wins elections in the evening then the burning coal is stuffed into their mouths. They keep crying. Their scream reaches to the village but nobody comes to help them. Their tongue and lips are melted away and ultimately they are killed by strangulating with the rope. Thakur becomes blind with the anger. Thakur's ager does not pacify with their death. He orders his goons to bring all of the members of Narayan's family and burns them alive. He wants to show his power to the poor dalits. He sends their dead bodies on the village square so that any other Dalit may not dare to speak against him. When Ishvar and Ashraf Chacha try to lodge an F.I.R.

against the real murderer, Thakur Dharamsi the inspector does not take any action rather he scolds them: What kind of rascality is this? Trying to fill up the F.I.R. with lies? You filth achoot caste are always out to make trouble! Get out before we charge you with public Mischief (172).

Dalits like Ishvar and Narayan are harshly punished for minor infractions—such as walking near temples or being curious about education. When Ishvar and Narayan sneak into a school out of a desire to learn, they are beaten mercilessly. Their family is then ostracized, showcasing how upper-caste power structures enforce subjugation. Narayan, Ishvar's brother, dares to challenge the status quo by becoming a tailor and demanding his right to vote. His defiance leads to horrifying consequences. During an election, when he insists on voting, he and other rebels are tortured and killed under orders from Thakur Dharamsi, a powerful upper-caste man. The violence escalates—Narayan's entire family is burned alive, including women and children. Mistry paints a chilling portrait of caste-based brutality that persists even in post-independence India.

Only Ishvar and Omprakash survive this atrocity. Attempting to seek justice, they are instead accused of causing public disorder. Mistry uses their story to expose the deep-rooted corruption in police and political systems, where victims are blamed and perpetrators are shielded. Even after fleeing their village, Ishvar and Omprakash face systemic discrimination. Ishvar and Narayan's experiences with caste-based abuse:

Chamaar's son trying to become a tailor? Next he will want to become prime minister! Teach him a lesson he will never forget.(150)

This line is directed at Narayan, Ishvar's brother, who dares to defy the caste hierarchy by entering a profession traditionally not allowed for someone of his caste. The quote reflects the deep-rooted prejudice and aggression from upper-caste individuals toward any form of upward mobility by Dalits. This moment encapsulates how any attempt by lower-caste individuals to better themselves—even through honest work—is perceived as a threat by the upper-caste elites, often met with violent retaliation.

Beyond the physical abuse and deprivation, *A Fine Balance* also emphasizes the emotional toll on its characters. Omprakash and Ishvar not only lose their families, homes, and bodies—they lose their futures. Maneck, a more privileged character, ultimately cannot cope with the overwhelming hopelessness around him and takes his own life. In contrast, the poor must continue to live through the pain, powerless but persistent. These invisible scars—the trauma, grief, shame, and numbness—remain long after the physical wounds have healed. Mistry shows that the true suffering of the underprivileged is not just what is seen, but what is silently endured.

Rohinton Mistry, through *A Fine Balance*, powerfully portrays the extreme hardships faced by the Dalits and other underprivileged groups in India. He critiques both caste-based and political oppression, illustrating how these forces intertwine to devastate lives. His narrative is a passionate call for human dignity, empathy, and justice—making him a powerful voice for the voiceless and a champion of human rights.

Works Cited

Chatterjee, Partha. *The Nation and Its Fragments: Colonial and Postcolonial Histories*. Princeton UP, 1993.

Mistry, Rohinton. *A Fine Balance*. Vintage Canada, 2001.

Nayar, Pramod K. *Contemporary Literary and Cultural Theory: From Structuralism to Ecocriticism*. Pearson Education India, 2010.

Omvedt, Gail. *Dalits and the Democratic Revolution: Dr. Ambedkar and the Dalit Movement in Colonial India*. Sage Publications, 1994.

Sivaramakrishnan, Arvind. "The Pain and the Balance." *The Hindu*, 16 Jan. 2000, www.thehindu.com.

Tharu, Susie, and K. Lalita, editors. *Women Writing in India: 600 B.C. to the Present*. Vol. 2, Feminist Press at CUNY, 1993.

CHAPTER TWENTY-SIX

Silenced No More: The Subaltern Speaks in Nawal El Saadawi's Woman at Point Zero

Dr.G.S.Chitra
Guest Lecturer, Department of English ,
Kalaignar Karunanidhi Government Arts College,
Tiruvannamalai, Tamilnadu. 606603

Abstract

Nawal El Saadawi's *Woman at Point Zero* (1975) is a seminal work in feminist and postcolonial literature that explores the intersections of gender, power, and systemic oppression. Based on the real-life account of a woman awaiting execution, the novel critiques patriarchal structures that perpetuate the subjugation of women. Firdaus, the protagonist, represents a voice of defiance against the institutionalized exploitation of women in Egyptian society. Through the novel's first-person narration, El Saadawi dismantles traditional narratives that romanticize women's suffering, instead presenting a stark and unfiltered critique of socio-economic hierarchies. This paper examines *Woman at Point Zero* through feminist and postcolonial theoretical frameworks, analyzing how the novel challenges hegemonic discourses on gender and power. By employing a non-linear storytelling technique and a deeply introspective narrative voice, El Saadawi reclaims the silenced experiences of marginalized women. The study highlights how Firdaus's journey from victimhood to resistance serves as a powerful indictment of patriarchal and capitalist oppression. Ultimately, the novel redefines notions of agency and justice, making it a critical text in feminist literary discourse.

Keywords: Feminism, Postcolonialism, Patriarchy, Gender Oppression, Agency, Resistance

Silenced No More: The Subaltern Speaks in Nawal El Saadawi's
Woman at Point Zero

Introduction

Nawal El Saadawi's *Woman at Point Zero* is a landmark novel that critiques the gendered structures of power in Egyptian society. The novel, based on a true story, presents the life of Firdaus, a woman who has suffered relentless abuse yet ultimately claims her autonomy in an act of radical resistance. Through the lens of feminism and postcolonialism, this paper explores how El Saadawi constructs a narrative that challenges dominant discourses on gender and power.

Gender Oppression and Systemic Violence

Firdaus's life is marked by multiple layers of oppression familial, societal, and institutional. As a child, she experiences neglect and abuse, highlighting the normalized violence against women in patriarchal households. Later, as she enters adulthood, she faces further subjugation through exploitative relationships and systemic coercion. El Saadawi's critique of gender-based oppression aligns with feminist theories that examine the ways in which patriarchy subordinates women. By exposing the harsh realities of prostitution and male entitlement, *Woman at Point Zero* dismantles the myth of female passivity and victimhood. As Firdaus declares in the novel, *"I have triumphed over both life and death because I no longer desire to live, nor do I any longer fear to die"* (El Saadawi 114). This statement encapsulates her defiance and ultimate liberation from societal control.

Feminist scholar Miriam Cooke argues that El Saadawi's novel *"challenges not only the patriarchal oppression of women but also the complicity of women who internalize and perpetuate these structures"* (Cooke 45). This perspective highlights how Firdaus's journey reflects broader struggles within feminist movements.

Postcolonial Readings: Resistance and Reclamation

As a postcolonial text, *Woman at Point Zero* situates Firdaus's oppression within broader socio-political contexts. The colonial legacy in Egypt exacerbates class disparities and economic disenfranchisement, further marginalizing women. Firdaus's resistance, particularly in her rejection of societal expectations, signifies an anti-colonial and feminist act. Her refusal to submit to oppressive structures echoes Frantz Fanon's assertion that decolonization is inherently violent, as the oppressed reclaim agency through radical means.

Literary critic Amal Amireh notes, *"El Saadawi's novel reconfigures the subaltern narrative by giving Firdaus a voice that is both personal and political, resisting not only patriarchal structures but also neocolonial influences that seek to control female bodies"* (Amireh 88).

The Role of Narrative Structure and Voice

El Saadawi employs a first-person narrative that immerses readers in Firdaus's psyche. The nonlinear structure, which interweaves past trauma with present reflections, mirrors Firdaus's fragmented identity shaped by years of subjugation. This narrative technique disrupts conventional storytelling and forces readers to confront the raw and unfiltered realities of oppression. Additionally, Firdaus's voice challenges male-centric narratives, asserting the validity of women's lived experiences in literary discourse. Gayatri Chakravorty Spivak's concept of *"can the subaltern speak?"* becomes relevant here, as Firdaus's testimony stands as an assertion of agency despite the systemic silencing of marginalized women (Spivak 104).

Firdaus as a Symbol of Radical Agency

Despite enduring immense suffering, Firdaus reclaims her power through an act of ultimate defiance—murdering a man who embodies patriarchal dominance. Her execution does not symbolize defeat but rather a triumph over societal control. By choosing death over submission, Firdaus transcends victimhood and redefines agency on her own terms. This radical assertion of autonomy challenges traditional feminist narratives that equate liberation with survival. Scholar Fadia Faqir emphasizes, *"Firdaus's rebellion is emblematic of a greater struggle against structures of control that regulate women's autonomy. Her decision to embrace death rather than subjugation marks a radical departure from conventional narratives of female empowerment"* (Faqir 72).

Conclusion

Saadawi's *Woman at Point Zero* is a powerful critique of patriarchal and colonial oppression, offering a harrowing yet empowering portrayal of female resistance. Through its bold narrative structure and unflinching depiction of gender-based violence, the novel forces readers to re-evaluate notions of justice and agency. Firdaus's story remains a testament to the resilience of marginalized women, making *Woman at Point Zero* an essential text in feminist and postcolonial literature.

Works Cited

Amireh, Amal. *"Framing Nawal El Saadawi: Arab Feminism in a Transnational World."* Signs: Journal of Women in Culture and Society, vol. 26, no. 1, 2000, pp. 87-112.

Cooke, Miriam. *Women Claim Islam: Creating Islamic Feminism through Literature.* Routledge, 2001.

El Saadawi, Nawal. *Woman at Point Zero.* Translated by Sherif Hetata, Zed Books, 1983.

Faqir, Fadia. *"Intricate Affiliations: Colonialism, Nationalism, and Gender in Arab Women's Novels."* Feminist Review, vol. 61, 1999, pp. 70-89.

Fanon, Frantz. *The Wretched of the Earth.* Grove Press, 1963.

Mohanty, Chandra Talpade. *Feminism Without Borders: Decolonizing Theory, Practicing Solidarity.* Duke University Press, 2003.

Spivak, Gayatri Chakravorty. *"Can the Subaltern Speak?"* Marxism and the Interpretation of Culture, edited by Cary Nelson and Lawrence Grossberg, University of Illinois Press, 1988, pp. 104-118.